Australian Heroines

Australian Heroines

stories of courage and survival

Susan Geason

ABC BOOKS

Published by ABC Books for the
AUSTRALIAN BROADCASTING CORPORATION
GPO Box 9994 Sydney NSW 2001

Copyright © Susan Geason 2001

First published 2001

All rights reserved. No part of this publication may be reproduced, stored in a retrieval system or transmitted in any form or by any means, electronic, mechanical, photocopying, recording or otherwise, without the prior written permission of the Australian Broadcasting Corporation.

National Library of Australia
Cataloguing-in-Publication entry
Geason, Susan, 1946– .
    Australian heroines : stories of courage and survival.

    Includes index.
    ISBN 0 7333 0966 6.

    1. Women heroes – Australia – Biography – Juvenile literature. 2. Women heroes – Australia – History – Juvenile literature. I. Australian Broadcasting Corporation. II. Title.

    920.720994

Designed by Kerry Klinner
Cover designed by Monkeyfish
Set in 12.5/16.5 Goudy Old Style by Asset Typesetting Pty Ltd, Sydney
Colour separations by Colorwize, Adelaide
Printed and bound in Australia by Griffin Press, Adelaide

5 4 3 2 1

*This book is dedicated
to my mother, Joan Geason,
whose courage inspires me,
and to my friend, Erna Nelson,
for her generosity and support.*

Contents

Mary Bryant
Escape from the End of the Earth   1
Who was Mary Bryant?   24

Truganini
Trekking the Wilds of Van Diemen's Land   30
The War Against the First Tasmanians   56
The Battle for the Bones   59

Barbara Crawford Thompson
Shipwrecked   61

Sarah White Musgrave
Sarah of the South-west Plains   82
Rewriting the Past   106

May Zinga Wirth
The Greatest Horsewoman on Earth   108

Molly Craig
Escape from the Moore River Native Settlement   129
The Desert Aborigines   153
The 'Stolen Children'   156

Marika Cierer Weinberger
Holocaust Survivor   166
The War Against the Jews   203

Brigitte Muir
The View from the Top of the World   211

Samantha Miles
Surviving a Life-threatening Illness   240

Susie Maroney
The Loneliness of the Long-distance Swimmer   263

Glossary   285

Sources   286

Index   293

Acknowledgments

For Mary Bryant — Robert Holden, Professor Alan Frost, C H Currey; for Molly Craig — Doris Pilkington; Emma Cooper, TheArcFactory; Christine Olsen, Olsen & Levy; University of Queensland Press; for Susie Maroney — Susie & Pauline Maroney; Professor John Carmody, Kenneth Graham & Dr Michael Martin, sports physiologists & John Crampton, Athlete Management Services, NSW Institute of Sport; for Samantha Miles — Samantha Miles; for Brigitte Muir — Brigitte & Jon Muir, Professor John Carmody; Penguin/Viking Books; for Sarah White Musgrave — Leon Isackson & Borise Hawtin, descendants; Barbara Brennan, Secretary, Young Historical Society; for Barbara Thompson — David Moore; for Truganini — Dr Lyndall Ryan; Tasmanian Land Council; Tasmanian Art Gallery & Museum; for Marika Weinberger — Marika Weinberger, Rabbi Jeffrey Cohen, Sydney Jewish Museum; for May Wirth — Geoff Greaves; Mark St Leon; Arthur Easton, Mitchell Library Manuscripts; Cate Jones, Australia Post.

Thank you to Ali Lavau and Lisa Riley at ABC Books, for scrupulous editing and unfailing good humour; David Francis and Matthew Kelly, ABC Books, for backing another project; and to the staff at the Mitchell Library and the Jessie Street Library; Paul Stanish; Anthea O'Brien, Erna Nelson, Patricia Nilvor, Simon Taaffe, Neil McDonell, Carmel Bird and Byron Addison.

Introduction

The girls and women in *Australian Heroines* come from different parts of the country, different historical periods, and very different backgrounds. What they have in common is their extraordinary courage and determination.

Some of the stories in the book chronicle amazing adventures. Mary Bryant escaped from Botany Bay in a glorified row-boat with her two small children, her husband and some fellow convicts, and sailed to Timor without the aid of charts or maps. May Wirth endured countless hours of training, aches and pains and falls to become a superstar in the world's greatest circus. Removed from their families in the Pilbara in Western Australia, Molly Craig and her cousins escaped from the Moore River Native Settlement near Perth and walked 1600 kilometres home dodging search parties. Susie Maroney kept ploughing through the water till she'd broken every marathon swimming record in the book. After conquering altitude sickness, dreadful cold, fatigue and self-doubt, Brigitte Muir reached the summit of Mount Everest and fulfilled her goal of climbing the highest mountain on each of the seven continents.

As well as adventures — feats of derring-do — there are astonishing survival stories in this book. Finding themselves in deep peril, these young women had to call on all the physical and emotional strength they possessed. After running away from home in Sydney, Barbara Thompson was shipwrecked on the Great Barrier Reef and spent years living on an island in Torres Strait with the Kaurareg tribe before being rescued by a ship from the British Navy. Recruited by George Robinson to help him negotiate a peace with her fellow Tasmanian Aborigines, Truganini spent years trekking the most inaccessible corners of the island's west coast with the so-called Friendly Mission. Born on an isolated property on New South Wales's south-west plains, Sarah Musgrave thrived on hard work and lived through drought, floods, bushrangers and a goldrush. Caught up in Adolf Hitler's campaign to murder all the Jews of Europe, Marika Weinberger survived concentration camps, forced marches, beatings and starvation before migrating to Australia to start a new life. With only three weeks to live when she was diagnosed with leukaemia, Samantha Miles fought like a tiger to overcome the illness and its physical and emotional after-effects.

Those of you who read *Great Australian Girls* and visited my website (www.susangeason.com) may have seen the explanatory essays I wrote to accompany the stories in that volume. This time we've included them in the book. You'll find a description of the white settlers' war against the Tasmanian Aborigines that puts Truganini's treks on the Friendly Mission in context, for example, and an essay on the 'stolen children' that helps explain Molly Craig's abduction and flight.

Writing this book and meeting some of my heroines has been quite an experience. With the surf pounding on the beach a hundred metres away, I had afternoon tea with Susie Maroney in her flat at Cronulla in Sydney's

Introduction

south. I visited the Sydney Jewish Museum twice and did eight hours of often emotional interviews with Marika Weinberger, making a new friend in the process. During the Olympic Games, I travelled to Waitara on Sydney's north shore in a hot, packed train full of exhausted sports fans, to be met by Samantha Miles at the station and whizzed through Galston Gorge in a sports car to her secluded house at Dural. I also made a flying visit to Natimuk — a speck on the map outside Horsham in Victoria's Wimmera district — to visit the home of Brigitte Muir, who kindly cooked me a vegetable and tofu stir-fry for dinner.

It's right to be inspired by these women and their stories of daring, courage and tenacity, but not to be overawed. We all know that ordinary people can do extraordinary things when they're put to the test. Obviously not everyone can take up mountaineering, turn backward somersaults on a galloping horse or swim from Cuba to Miami, but we can all learn to stand up for ourselves, push our minds and bodies to the limit and reach our potential. We can take risks, chase our dreams and become our own heroine. We can be brave.

Mary Bryant

Escape from the End of the Earth

Mary Bryant escaping with other convicts from Port Jackson in 1791.
Illustration by Francis J. Broadhurst, reproduced from C H Currey's
The Transportation, Escape and Pardoning of Mary Bryant (1983)

Transported to New South Wales for seven years for theft, Mary Bryant escaped from Botany Bay in a small sailboat with her husband, her two children and seven other convicts. They reached Kupang in West Timor, but were captured. Though Mary's husband and two small children perished on the journey back to London, she survived. After a year in Newgate Prison, she was freed by a public campaign led by the lawyer and writer, James Boswell.

Mary Broad was born in Fowey in Cornwall in 1765, the daughter of a sailor. In earlier times, she might have lived out her life in this tiny fishing village, but in the late eighteenth century thousands of people left the English countryside and flooded into the cities looking for a better life. Some found it; others found only trouble. Mary Broad was part of this exodus, moving to Plymouth, the biggest city in Cornwall and a base for the ships of the Royal Navy's western fleet, which patrolled the English Channel and the Atlantic Ocean.

Mary quickly discovered that town life could be hard and unforgiving. There were two distinct societies in England: the rich and the poor. For the poor, jobs were hard to come by, and there was no welfare. Those who could not find work had to beg, steal or starve. Perhaps Mary could not find a position as a maid, or perhaps she was fired from her job, but somehow she ended up thieving to survive. In Mary's day, this was a dangerous occupation. Private property was sacred, and stealing was punished with the full force of the law. Offenders, including women and children, could be hanged for crimes such as horse theft, fraud or counterfeiting money. Despite this, crime was rife. As there was some safety in numbers, Mary formed a gang with two other women, Catherine Fryer and Mary Haydon. Once they'd spotted a victim, one woman would stand lookout, another would distract the victim, and the third would grab a purse, a shawl, a hat or a parcel — then they would all run off. In 1786 the inevitable happened: Mary and her accomplices assaulted Agnes Lakeman, a 'spinster', stealing her silk bonnet and jewellery, and were caught.

Grey-eyed with a sallow complexion, and only 162 centimetres tall, 21-year-old Mary Broad stood in the dock at the Exeter Assizes and listened with disbelief as the judge, resplendent in a horsehair wig and flowing robes, sentenced her to hanging. In fact, most offenders were not hanged, and Mary's sentence was commuted to transportation for seven years. Ten years earlier, she would have been shipped to one of the American colonies, but after the Americans won their independence from Britain in 1776, they refused to take any more of the old country's cast-offs. Desperate for somewhere to house convicts, the authorities began using hulks — old warships moored in rivers and at sea — as makeshift prisons. Mary was consigned to the *Dunkirk*, a hulk moored off Plymouth. She was lucky. Once a den of lawlessness and depravity, by then the *Dunkirk* had been taken over by the Admiralty and cleaned up. On the *Dunkirk* Mary met three men who would play a pivotal role in her life — William Bryant, James Martin and James Cox. One of them, Will Bryant, a 27-year-old fisherman from Cornwall imprisoned for receiving smuggled goods, became her lover.

While Mary languished on the *Dunkirk*, the government began planning to transport prisoners to Botany Bay in New Holland (now Australia). It was a radical and risky move; New Holland was largely unknown territory. Captain James Cook had reported favourably on Botany Bay and the east coast on his expedition in 1770, but very little of the continent had been explored or charted by Europeans. Botany Bay was on the other side of the world, nine months from England by sea. Of the 729 convicts selected to be part of this experiment, 200 of them — including 41 women — came from the *Dunkirk*. Mary, along with Bryant, Martin and Cox, was assigned to the

Mary Bryant

Charlotte, one of the eleven ships that made up the First Fleet.

Waiting to board the ship at Plymouth docks, shivering in her rags, Mary Broad gazed around her. The fellow travellers she saw were a sorry lot — filthy, undernourished scarecrows, shivering, ragged and afraid. Fortunately for these outcasts, Captain Arthur Phillip had been put in charge of the fleet. He had the prisoners washed and deloused, fattened up, and properly clothed before they put to sea. It wasn't just compassion; Phillip knew that clean and healthy prisoners were more likely to survive the long sea voyage than these human wrecks from the festering jails and hulks of England.

Mary Broad left England aboard the *Charlotte* on 13 May 1787. With her, she carried a secret — but it could not stay secret for long. On 8 September 1787, with the fleet moored off Rio de Janeiro in South America, she gave birth to a baby girl she called Charlotte Spence. Spence was a convict Mary had known on the hulk — it's unknown whether he or Will Bryant was Charlotte's father.

It was a long and arduous journey for a pregnant woman. Shut up in the foetid air below decks, Mary suffered seasickness and morning sickness, nauseated by the stench of unwashed bodies and vomit. Even worse was the anguish of knowing she would probably never see her home and family again. When storms lashed the ship far from land, she sobbed in terror and wondered if she and her baby would live to see Botany Bay. But they did survive, and Mary impressed the ship's surgeon with her good behaviour.

When the *Charlotte* surged through Sydney Heads in January 1788, eight and a half months after leaving England, Mary, clutching her baby, joined the other curious convicts on deck. The sight that met her eyes was breathtaking: an enormous harbour with sapphire blue water, sandy inlets and wooded headlands. But it was a shock to a young woman who had never ventured beyond a small patch of England. Where Cornwall was green, this land was blue-grey. Instead of the pale, cloudy northern light of home, this light was bright and painful to the eye. Strange birdcalls, like mechanical laughter, rose up from the bushland on the shores. And where January in Cornwall brought fogs and chill, here the sun shone relentlessly from a perfect blue sky. But what was even more frightening was the emptiness. There was no sign of human habitation here; no buildings, crops, roads, bridges — not even a grass hut.

On 23 January, the fleet reached Botany Bay. But when Arthur Phillip realised there was no sheltered anchor and not enough fresh water, he led a scouting party on a search for a better landing place. They found Sydney Cove, and on 26 January the fleet

Mary Bryant

landed there. While the women waited on board, the men went ashore and began clearing the land for a settlement, cutting down trees and putting up tents. Only then were the women allowed to disembark and assigned their places in the tents.

Released from months of imprisonment, boredom and anxiety, the convicts held a wild, all-night party. For the first time in months, the men and women were allowed to mix. A violent summer storm capped off the celebrations, drenching the revellers and turning the ground to mud. Watching from the shelter of the bush, the Aborigines thought they were seeing ghosts rolling around in the mud. If the Aborigines were astonished, the more staid members of the landing party were shocked by the convicts' behaviour. The next day Governor Phillip cracked down. It was his job to make the settlement self-supporting, and that meant order, discipline and hard work. From now on, anyone who broke the rules would be severely punished.

But how did you create a normal society out of such a motley crew? There were men, women and children of all ages. Some were fit; others were weak from a lifetime of bad food, poor housing and hard work. Some could read and write; others were illiterate. Few had the practical skills needed to carve a living out of this wilderness. But most of them had one thing in common: they had been forced to leave their families behind. Distraught widows had been dragged away from their children, leaving them to an uncertain fate on the streets of the towns and cities. Children as young as eleven had been transported without their parents. Wives and husbands were separated from each other and from their children. Nowhere else on earth did such an unnatural society exist. Believing it would lead to trouble, Governor Phillip decided to encourage normal family life. By the end of February thirty couples had wed, including Mary Broad and William Bryant.

In the circumstances, Mary made a good choice in Will. He was a fisherman, and the colony sorely needed to feed all those empty stomachs. Put in charge of the fishing fleet, Will quickly became indispensable. He was given a hut and allowed to keep some of the fish he caught. Compared to most of the convicts, Will and his family lived in relative luxury. Unfortunately, Will could not resist temptation, and began selling fish on the black market. The word got out, and Will was tried, found guilty and given 100 lashes with the cat, a knotted whip made of strong twine. The Bryants were thrown out of their hut and Mary had to move back into a tent with the baby. Though he was allowed to continue fishing, Will was relieved of command of the fishing fleet. Despite his fall from grace, he was defiant. He started thinking about escape.

Mary Bryant

Convicts in New Holland by Juan Ravenet, 1793. Courtesy Mitchell Library, State Library of New South Wales.

Meanwhile, the colony's supplies were running low. Famine was a very real threat. Alarmed, the Governor sent the man-of-war *Sirius* to the Cape of Good Hope in October, and the *Supply*, an armed tender, to Batavia to buy provisions. To ease the pressure on the food supply until they returned, he loaded the ships with a detachment of marines and 200 convicts to be put ashore at Norfolk Island en route. Tragically, the *Sirius* was wrecked after offloading its passengers. To make matters worse, the *Guardian*, on its way from England laden with supplies, hit an iceberg off the coast of South Africa in December and had to limp back to Table Bay.

After the loss of the *Sirius*, rations were cut drastically. Adults and children over 18 months had to survive on weekly rations of less than a kilogram of old, tough salt pork and the same quantity of weevilly rice, a little over a kilogram of flour, and about a kilogram of peas. Then drought struck and the vegetable plants withered in the parched ground. People grew gaunt and frightened. It was in April of this terrible year, 1790 — 'the starving time' — that Mary's son Emanuel was born. To add to the colony's woes, the *Lady Juliana* arrived in June carrying 221 female convicts and eleven children, and not enough provisions to feed them. It was quickly followed by three transports from the Second Fleet, carrying 759 convicts — 486 of them sick — and the first detachment of the New South Wales Marine Corps, who would police the colony.

The situation eased when the *Justinian*, the Second Fleet's storeship, arrived in Botany Bay loaded to the gunwales with supplies. But by this time many of the convicts had had enough; they decided to get out of this God-forsaken place before they perished. In September, five desperadoes from Rose Hill — now Parramatta — seized a boat and set out for Tahiti. (They reached Port Stephens, where four of them were picked up five years later.) Security was tightened, but this didn't deter those determined to leave. Mary and Will and several of their friends began to plot their escape. This would be no ordinary jail break. Australia was a huge prison surrounded by a moat — they would have to escape by sea. That meant getting hold of a boat. Will bided his time.

Meanwhile, the endless search for food went on. Every boat in the colony was put to work fishing. Every able-bodied person, high and low, pitched in to help. Even army officers, public servants, doctors and a clergyman had to learn how to bait a hook and cast a line. Once again Will's skill as a fisherman proved invaluable. The Bryants were given back their hut.

In October the *Supply* returned from Batavia with a small cargo of food. While in Indonesia, its captain had hired a Dutch ship, the *Waaksamheyd*, to bring provisions to Botany Bay. When it docked, Will made contact with the captain, Detmer Smit — a hard, unscrupulous man with no qualms about selling forbidden goods to convicts — and bought a compass and a quadrant for navigating, a chart, two muskets, ammunition and food.

The authorities were aware that Will and his friends were planning to abscond — someone had overheard them plotting — and the marines placed them under surveillance. Then fate stepped in and helped the conspirators: a squall swamped the Governor's six-oared cutter. This was the boat Will had been waiting for. Given the job of overhauling it, he secretly prepared it for a voyage to Timor with a new mast, and new sails and oars.

As soon as darkness fell on 28 March 1791, William Bryant and his accomplices — William Allen, John Butcher (also known as Samuel Broom), James Cox, Nathaniel Lilley, James Martin, William Morton and John Simms (alias Samuel Bird) — began carrying the supplies to the boat and secreting them on board, taking care not to be seen. At about 11 p.m. on that moonless night they set off from Port Jackson, near Mrs Macquarie's Point, in the Governor's boat. With them were Mary Bryant and her two small children — Charlotte, now three and a half, and Emanuel, 12 months. Stowed on board were 45 kilograms of flour, 36 litres of water, a new fishing net, cooking utensils, fishing lines and hooks, and two muskets and ammunition. To help them navigate they had the compass, quadrant and chart Will had bought from Captain Smit. Mary had also packed some of the sarsaparilla leaves the convicts used for making a nutritious drink called 'sweet tea'.

They cast off quietly, keeping watch for prying eyes. Soon they were out in the harbour, making for the Heads before sailing north up the coast of New South Wales. Will had planned well: because the Dutch ship had sailed and the *Supply* had left for Norfolk Island, there were no vessels in the harbour capable of chasing and catching them.

Mary was on tenterhooks. As a sailor's daughter, she was not afraid of boats, but she knew this would be a long, difficult and dangerous voyage. What if the charts were wrong? What if they ran into storms and high seas? Were there pirates in these waters? She consoled herself with the thought that five of the men had sailing experience, and more importantly, that William Morton was a trained navigator. Mary knew the risks — if they were caught, she and Will could be hanged — but she chose freedom. She couldn't let Charlotte and Emanuel starve in Botany Bay or grow up tainted by their parents' criminal pasts.

When the Bryants and their friends did not appear next morning, the alarm was raised. The marines realised what had happened when they found a handsaw, a scale and a bag of rice at the

Point. A search of the Bryants' hut uncovered a hiding place under the floor where contraband goods had been stashed. A party of marines set out to look for them in the long boat, but could not catch them. By this time, the cutter had reached the ocean and was heading north.

The voyage took a physical and emotional toll on the escapees. For the first five weeks it rained steadily. Storms hit the little boat, tossing it around like a cork. Torrential rains drenched them repeatedly. After one gale, the boat leaked so badly and sat so low in the water that they had to throw their clothes overboard to lighten the load, or sink. Water was a constant problem. At one stage they were out of sight of land for three weeks and came close to dying of thirst.

Apart from thirst, their greatest danger was the Aborigines. Never knowing if Aborigines were hidden in the bush watching their every move, they had to be constantly on their guard. The Aborigines at Newcastle were curious rather than hostile, and went away happily when the convicts gave them some clothes. But farther north, when they moored in a fine harbour to collect fresh water, the Aborigines attacked. When Will fired his musket over the warriors' heads, they retreated. On another occasion, when the convicts chased two Aboriginal women out of their gunyahs, a party of warriors came after the fugitives and drove them off.

Mary Bryant

The voyage wasn't all hardship. Life on the open sea was bracing and healthy, and the convicts exulted in the freedom of escaping from Botany Bay and its horrible memories. Mary saw places where no white people had been before. Sometimes they would put ashore to dry out sails, caulk seams, and refill their water tanks. The men would catch fish and Mary would cook them on an open fire on the beach. On one of the Whitsunday Islands on the Great Barrier Reef they found turtles, turned them over and cooked them, drying some of the turtle meat over the fire for later. They also discovered mutton-birds living in nests in the ground, and were unnerved by their mournful wailing calls. As they sailed north, food became scarce, and they would have starved without the dried turtle and some shellfish they collected from little coral islands. In the Gulf of Carpentaria, they had their most dangerous encounter with the traditional owners of the land. Alerted to the presence of strangers in their territory, a party of Torres Strait Islanders came speeding towards them in two canoes. Alarmed, Will shot over their heads, and the islanders retreated. Believing they were safe, the convicts landed to get water, then moored off the coast. But next morning two war canoes appeared, each bearing thirty to forty men armed with spears. Outnumbered, the escapees had to pull up the anchor and outrun them. It took four and a half hot, thirsty days to reach the other side of the Gulf.

After clearing Arnhem Land, Mary and her party faced the most dangerous leg of the voyage — the long run to Timor. This was where William Morton proved his value — a skilled navigator, he brought them through the Arafura Sea safely without charts. After coasting along the southern edge of the island of Timor, they tied up at the wharf in Kupang on 5 June 1791. They had been at sea for sixty-nine days, and had sailed over 5000 kilometres. This extraordinary voyage has gone down in seafaring history. And though they were sunburnt, ragged and thin, Mary, Charlotte and Emanuel were all in good health; in fact, they'd weathered the voyage better than some of the men.

In Timor the escapees posed as survivors of a shipwrecked whaling vessel. The Governor of the Dutch colony took pity on them and treated them well. Some of the men found work, and Mary and the children idled away their time in the picturesque town. But it was too good to last. Now that he was free, Will let down his guard and talked about his plans for the future. When Mary realised that they did not include her and the children, that Will did not consider his colonial marriage binding, they fought. Will drowned his sorrows in rum and let his tongue run away with him. Their secret was out.

Mary Bryant

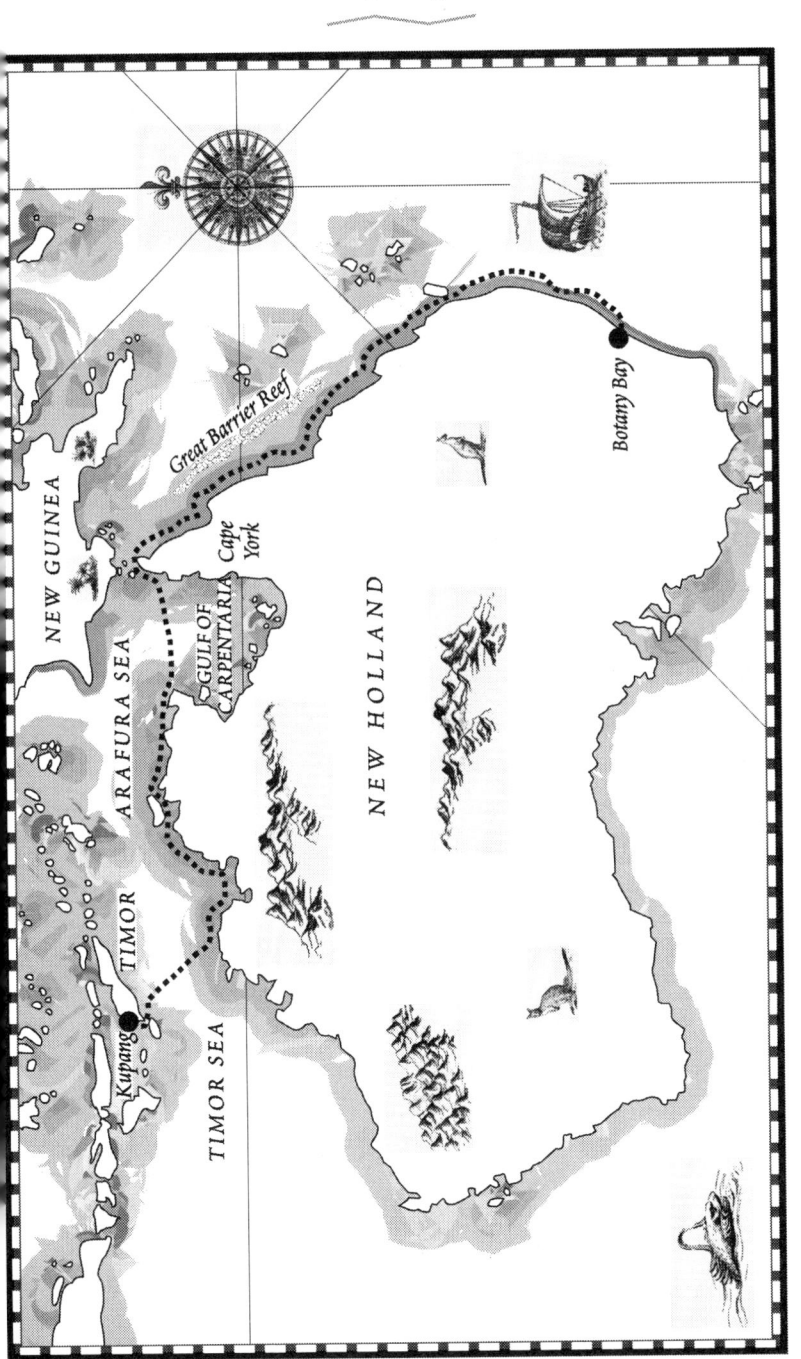

The route taken by Mary and Will Bryant and their fellow convicts on their daring escape from Botany Bay in 1791. Map drawn by Stanish Graphics.

Once the Governor knew they were escaped convicts, he had no choice but to put them in prison. But because he was a kind man and admired their courage in escaping from Botany Bay, he allowed them to come and go from the jail during the day.

This easygoing arrangement came to an abrupt end when the Royal Navy's Captain Edward Edwards turned up. Edwards had been sent out to the Friendly Islands of the South Seas in the *Pandora* to round up the sailors who had mutinied on Captain Bligh's ship, the *Bounty*, in 1790. He found some of the mutineers in Tahiti, but as he was bringing them in, his ship was wrecked in a cyclone in the Endeavour Straits on the northern end of the Great Barrier Reef. The survivors had rowed all the way to Timor in lifeboats.

A cold, hard man, Captain Edwards had no sympathy for escaped convicts. After interrogating the Bryants and their friends, he clapped them in irons and sent them to Batavia on board the *Rembang*. After weathering a cyclone on the way, the prisoners were incarcerated on a Dutch guard ship while Edwards made arrangements for transporting them to England. Notorious as a graveyard for white people, Batavia lived up to its name. On 1 December 1791 Emanuel Bryant died of fever, and twenty-one days later, typhus took his father, William. Distraught, Mary clung to Charlotte and prayed.

Mary Bryant

Finally, space was found for the escapees on Dutch ships — Mary, Charlotte and William Allen on the *Horssen*, and the others on the *Hoornwey*. These vessels were crowded and disease-ridden. On the journey, James Cox either fell overboard or jumped, hoping to swim to land. Weighed down by his leg iron, he drowned. John Simms and William Morton, the navigator, grew ill and died of fever. At Table Bay, Edwards and the escapees were transferred to the *Gorgon*, which was on its way back from Botany Bay to England with a cargo of strange animals and birds, and a deck full of exotic bushes and plants. The escapees had come full circle. The marines on the *Gorgon* immediately recognised the convicts — their daring escape had been the talk of the colony — and praised their bravery and seamanship. As James Martin wrote in an account of his adventure: 'We was well known by all the marine officers, which was all glad that we had not perished at sea.'

There were marines' wives and children on board the ship, but Mary was the only convict woman. Soon the women would have something in common. Five of the marine officers' children died, and on 6 May 1792, after surviving the harsh conditions in the colony and a dangerous voyage in an open boat, little Charlotte Spence succumbed to fever and died. Mary had lost everything: her husband, both her children and her freedom. And once she reached England, she would be very lucky to escape with her life.

The *Gorgon* anchored at Portsmouth on 18 June 1792, five years after Mary and Will had sailed for Botany Bay on the *Charlotte*. The escapees were brought before a magistrate, who committed them to Newgate Prison. He did so reluctantly; perhaps he thought they'd been through enough. On 7 July they appeared in the dock at the Old Bailey. It was a very different Mary Bryant from the girl who'd fronted the court in Plymouth six years before. She was now 27, and sorrow, privation and months in an open boat had etched new lines on her face. The judge did not impose the full penalty under the law — death — but ruled that the convicts should keep serving their original sentences until the courts saw fit to discharge them.

Mary went back to Newgate. Though the worst section of this notorious prison had burned down and been rebuilt, it was still filthy, crowded, and violent. Mourning the loss of her children and her husband, and perhaps facing years in hell, Mary scarcely noticed her surroundings.

While the absconders were languishing in the worst jail in Britain, the newspapers were turning them into celebrities. The law might take a dim view of escaping from Botany Bay, but the public found the story irresistible. The *Dublin Chronicle* of 21 July

1792 called the escape 'the most hazardous and wonderful effort ever made by nine persons (sic) (for two were infants) to regain their liberty.'

Though Mary was unaware of it in the bowels of Newgate, this blaze of publicity would be her salvation, for it attracted the interest of James Boswell. The well-known author of *Travels in the Hebrides* and the biography of Samuel Johnson (the famous writer, critic and conversationalist), Boswell had moved to London from Edinburgh to try to make his name as a lawyer. He did not make much money as a lawyer, but he did gain a reputation for winning difficult cases. After interviewing the returned convicts in Newgate, he decided to take up their cause. He began to agitate for their release, laying siege to Evan Nepean, the English Secretary of State. It was a long campaign — Nepean resisted because he did not want to encourage other convicts to escape — but eventually it bore fruit. On 2 May 1793, Mary Broad, as she called herself once more, was granted an unconditional pardon and discharged from prison, six weeks after her original seven-year sentence had expired.

Mary stayed in London until the following October. Boswell and his friends helped her, giving her money for such necessities as a bonnet, a gown, shoes and a prayer book. After reading about Mary in the newspapers, a glazier who'd lived in Fowey came forward and told Boswell he knew Mary's sister, Dolly, who was a maid in London. Mary was reunited with Dolly, who assured her the family wanted her back. Keen to remove Mary from the dangers and temptations of life in the city, Boswell encouraged her to return to Fowey. Mary was ambivalent. In a huge city like London, she could disappear into anonymity; how would she be treated in a small town where everybody knew her story? And how would she fare without Boswell's protection? He eventually got his way by bribing Mary. He promised to pay her fare to Fowey and send her ten pounds a year as long as she behaved herself. Mary accepted the offer.

On 12 October 1793, James Boswell and his son picked Mary up from her lodgings in Little Titchfield Street in a hackney coach. As the horses clip-clopped through the twisting, cobbled streets, Mary took her last look at London. Their destination was Beale's Wharf in Southwark, where Mary was to board the *Ann and Elizabeth* for the voyage home. At Southwark Mary and Boswell whiled away two hours talking and drinking punch in the pub at the wharf with the ship's captain. Mary tried to keep up a good front, but she was miserable. She'd enjoyed being feted as a brave adventurer and had relished the attention of a man as famous as James Boswell; now she was anxious about the reception she'd get from her family and her neighbours in Fowey. Then it was time to go. They shook hands and Boswell watched Mary board the vessel. It was the last time they would ever see each other: Mary's saviour had only two more years to live. And Mary? The following year, Boswell paid five pounds of his own money into the bank account of the parish priest in a town near Fowey for Mary — after that she vanishes into obscurity.

After being released from Newgate, Mary had told her story to Boswell, who wrote it down. Sadly, these papers have never been found. But in 1937, a researcher found among Boswell's papers the sarsaparilla leaves Mary had kept as a souvenir from her remarkable journey. They are now in the Mitchell Library in Sydney.

Who was Mary Bryant?

How do you write about someone as far away in place and time as Mary Bryant? How do you discover the facts of her life? And, just as importantly, how do you get a sense of who she was, of what she was like?

In the case of Mary Bryant — also known as Mary Broad and Mary Braunt — the 'facts' took a long time to emerge. Some were easy to establish. We know her year of birth from her baptism certificate dated 1 May 1765, and we know that she was sentenced to hang for highway robbery, and that this was commuted to seven years' transportation, from records of the Exeter Assizes for the year 1786. She appears on First Fleet documents recording convicts sailing for Botany Bay on the *Charlotte* on 13 May 1787. The journal of the ship's doctor records the birth of her daughter, Charlotte, off Rio de Janeiro on 8 September 1787. Surgeon-General White also recorded that Mary was well-behaved on the voyage. The colony's Book of Registrations records the marriage of Mary and Will Bryant on 10 February 1788.

The escapees' recapture, and the deaths of Will Bryant, Charlotte and Emanuel (Mary's two children), John Simms, William Morton and James Cox were written up by Captain Edward Edwards of the Royal Navy, forwarded to the Admiralty in London, and then to Governor Phillip in Botany Bay in July 1792. From the newspapers of the day — for example, the *Dublin Chronicle* of 21 July and the *London Chronicle* in June and July 1792 — we have an account of the escape, the voyage and the recapture. A brief log of the voyage was later written down by James Martin in a little book called *Memorandoms*. In 1792 Watkin Tench — a marine officer who, by some quirk of fate, was not only on the *Charlotte* with Mary on the way to Botany Bay, but was also on the *Gorgon* which conveyed her back to jail in London — told the whole story in a book about the early days of New South Wales. Mary's pardon, dated 2 May 1793, is also on the public record.

This evidence was available to writers and historians, but that did not stop them getting the facts wrong. Stories about Mary misrepresent her age, the colour of her eyes and the circumstances of her arrest. Then, in 1885, two Sydney novelists read about Mary in George Barton's book, *The History of New South Wales through the Records*, and invented a new past for her. In their novel, *A First Fleet Family*, they made Mary's father an army lieutenant instead of a fisherman. They married her off to Watkin Tench in England and gave her three children instead of two and mixed up Charlotte and Emanuel's ages. They even had her arrested for trying to help her lover, Will Bryant, escape from

Winchester Prison, where he was serving a sentence for smuggling. All this is nonsense, but the novel was popular in London and New York, and many of its flights of fancy found their way into later books about Mary.

Interest in Mary's story revived in the 1930s. First, in 1937, Charles Blount found a copy of *Memorandoms*, James Martin's handwritten account of the escape, among the papers of the English philosopher Jeremy Bentham. It placed the blame for the betrayal of the escapees in Kupang on Will Bryant. The next year Frederick Pottle, an American scholar, published a slim volume called *Boswell and the Girl from Botany Bay*. Reading the papers and letters of the eighteenth-century Scottish writer and lawyer, James Boswell — which had only been made public in 1934 — Pottle realised that Boswell was the influential man who had championed the convicts and secured a pardon for Mary. And from Boswell's papers, we learn that Mary was reunited with her sister Dolly in London and returned to Fowey and her family late in 1793. Unfortunately, Pottle repeats some of the mistakes in *A First Fleet Family* — which someone showed him just before he published his book — as did Australian writer Geoffrey Rawson in *The Strange Case of Mary Bryant*, published in 1939.

Historian Charles Currey corrected many of these mistakes in *The Transportation, Escape and Pardoning* of Mary Bryant (née Broad) in 1963. He also placed Will on board the *Dunkirk* with Mary, reopening the question of who Charlotte's father was. But not even Currey could winkle out the legendary lost document — Mary's version of the story, which, according to Boswell, she dictated after her release from Newgate Prison.

As you can see, getting the facts right is difficult enough: getting into Mary's head is even harder. With no testament from Mary, we are forced to rely on the known facts and her actions to gauge her character and motives. We know she was a fisherman's daughter from Cornwall. Raised in a small, tightly knit community, she would have been used to hard work and danger — the men had to go out in all weathers in flimsy boats to make a living; the women had to wait at home and often bring up their children alone. To make ends meet, some Cornish fishermen resorted to smuggling. What this tells us is that Mary would have been brought up poor, proud and independent and without a great deal of respect for the law.

We don't know why Mary left Fowey, her home village, and moved to Plymouth — a broken love affair, or a desire to escape the poverty and drudgery of a fishing village, perhaps. Her descent into crime remains a mystery, too. Did she try being a servant and hate it? Did she steal from an employer and get the sack? Without a good reference, it would have been impossible to get a respectable job. And having left her own parish in Fowey, Mary would not have qualified for any assistance. To survive, she would have had to prostitute herself on the streets, beg, or steal. Mary chose to steal. From this, we know Mary was determined to survive on her own terms. Unfortunately for her, Mary was not a successful thief. At 21, she was sentenced to death, then transportation, for highway robbery.

Given what we already know about her, we're not surprised when Mary chooses to brave the open seas with Will and his friends — and her small children — rather than face starvation in Botany Bay. Again, she weathered the arduous journey well. And then it all began to fall apart. Mary and Will began arguing, according to James Martin, who had been their friend since the days on the *Dunkirk*. He says Will betrayed the escapees after an argument with Mary. What were they arguing about? Charles Currey speculates that Will let Mary know he didn't regard their colonial marriage as binding. With two small children to look after, Mary would have felt used, betrayed — and angry. That version of events rang true to me, probably because it fitted my mental image of Will (which is most likely completely inaccurate!) as dark, strong and a good leader, but also lawless and impulsive.

Mary Bryant

Like everyone else who's ever written about Mary, I'd like to know what happened to her after she returned to her family in Fowey. Unfortunately, she disappeared without trace a year after her return, when she received five pounds from James Boswell to help her go straight. I can't see Mary getting into any more trouble with the law after her experiences, but neither can I imagine her as a penitent spinster. If she found Fowey too small and judgmental after her notorious career, she may have migrated to America. If not, she probably married again and had more children. One day some clue to her fate might turn up.

Truganini

Trekking the Wilds of Van Diemen's Land

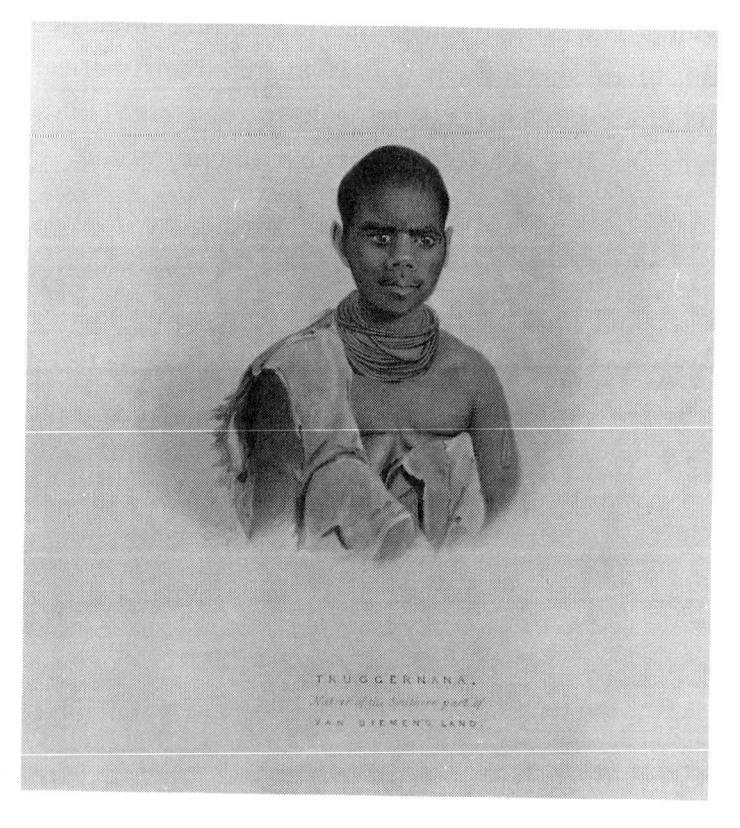

Trugnernana, Native of the Southern Part of Van Diemen's Land, watercolour by Thomas Bock, 1837. Collection Tasmanian Art Gallery & Museum.

Truganini

At the height of the war between the Tasmanian Aborigines and the white settlers in the 1820s, a 17-year-old Aboriginal girl called Truganini joined George Augustus Robinson on the 'Friendly Mission', a series of arduous and often dangerous expeditions into the wildest reaches of the island. It was Truganini's job to find Aborigines and try to talk them into ceasing hostilities against the whites. Though she is a controversial figure, there is no doubt about Truganini's extraordinary courage, physical strength and endurance, and her exceptional bushcraft.

The daughter of Mangerner, a chief of the Nuenonne, Truganini was born on Bruny Island around 1812. There were about seventy people in the Nuenonne, which was a band of the south-east tribal group. Until the arrival of the British in 1803, Truganini's people had lived a traditional Aboriginal life. They were nomadic, moving constantly around Bruny Island and making frequent trips in bark canoes to Oyster Cove, North West Bay and Recherche Bay to gather food and to socialise with other tribal bands.

Their diet consisted mainly of shellfish (fish with scales were taboo), swans' eggs, emu, kangaroo, wallaby, mutton-bird, witchetty grubs, and plants and yams. The women did most of the hard work, fetching and carrying, looking after the children, and preparing the food. This included diving for crayfish and shellfish, and catching possums by climbing tall trees using ropes made of kangaroo sinews.

By the time Truganini was born, white settlers were moving across Van Diemen's Land, fencing off traditional hunting grounds and driving the Aborigines out. Plagued by violence, starvation and the break-up of families, bands and tribes, Aboriginal society began to break down. The Aborigines on Bruny Island did not escape the chaos. When Truganini was very young, her family was attacked by white men, who stabbed her mother to death. Then, when she was about sixteen, her blood sister, Moorina, and two tribal sisters were abducted and taken to Kangaroo Island off the coast of South Australia. The following year, Truganini's step-mother was abducted by a party of mutinying convicts and taken away by ship, never to be seen again, and her brother Robert became ill and died.

Truganini's fiancé Paraweena was also murdered by white men, this time in a fight over Truganini. Jealous of the time Truganini was spending with convict sawyers at the timber works at Birch's Bay,

Truganini

Paraweena and a friend went to the mainland to bring her home. The convicts let Truganini go, and offered to row the three Aborigines home. Halfway across the channel, the men attacked Paraweena and his friend and threw them overboard. The Aboriginal men were good swimmers, however, and soon overtook the boat. But when they tried to climb aboard, one of the convicts picked up a tomahawk and cut off their hands. Paraweena and his friend fell back into the water and drowned. The convicts took Truganini back to Birch's Bay and sexually assaulted her. They were never punished.

When Truganini was 17, George Augustus Robinson arrived on Bruny Island. Robinson, an ambitious Yorkshireman, had won the contract to supply the remaining members of the Nuenonne with groceries and clothing. By this time, only nineteen Aborigines still lived on the island; among them were Truganini, her father Mangerner, two young women — Dray and Pagerly — and the warrior Woorraddy and his wife and three sons.

Unlike some of the mainland tribes who were locked into battle over territory with the whites, the Nuenonne were generally on good terms with the newcomers. They helped fishing crews and whalers, and were paid with tea and sugar. But when Robinson, who was a religious man, found out that Truganini, Dray and Pagerly were mixing with the convicts and whalers, he whisked them off to Hobart Town, out of harm's way, to stay with his long-suffering wife. Tiny Truganini, who stood only 130 centimetres tall, and was beautiful and clever, became a celebrity in Hobart. She was even invited to Government House to meet David Collins, the Lieutenant-Governor.

Robinson was determined to convert the Aborigines to Christianity and force them to behave like white people. He made them wear clothes and live in houses, and took the children away from their parents and put them into school. These changes wreaked havoc with the Aborigines' health and wellbeing. Wearing clothes that got wet and held the damp made them vulnerable to colds and chest infections. Prevented from foraging for healthy foods, they had to live on stodgy, unhealthy convict rations — bread, potatoes, biscuits, salt meat and tobacco. They began to fall sick and die. Those who were still healthy fled into the bush.

Truganini was lucky. Blessed with a strong constitution, she was immune to the bronchitis that killed so many of her people. By September 1829 only she, Mangerner, Woorraddy and his three sons, Dray, Pagerly and two orphan children, Joe and Morley, were left alive on Bruny Island. Woorraddy, a skilled hunter and storyteller, and a loyal friend of Robinson's, set his sights on Truganini after his young wife died in 1829. Truganini resisted being married off to a man twice her age, but George Robinson promoted the marriage because he liked Woorraddy and wanted to see Truganini settle down. In January 1830, after Truganini's father died and left her orphaned, she gave in and married Woorraddy. Soon after, Robinson closed the Aboriginal station and took the survivors back to Hobart, housing them next door to his family home.

In the meantime, conflict between the white settlers and the Aborigines was escalating. Determined to make a fortune and a name for himself in Van Diemen's Land, Robinson convinced Governor George Arthur that he could solve the problem peacefully. He believed he could talk the free Aborigines — those who lived beyond the frontier of white settlement — into coming out of the bush and moving onto a mission. The fact that most of the Aborigines on his own mission had died did not deter Robinson. His secret weapon would be the Bruny Island Aborigines, who he would use as go-betweens — or as some people dubbed them, 'black decoys'. At his wits' end, Arthur agreed to finance an expedition to the wild, unexplored west coast of Van Diemen's Land. This expedition became known as the Friendly Mission. It was the first attempt by a white man to negotiate a peaceful settlement with the Tasmanian Aborigines.

The first phase of the Mission would be a trek from Recherche Bay to Port Davey to make contact with the island's south-west tribe. Since the arrival of white people in their territory seven years before, this tribe had shrunk from between two to three hundred people to about sixty; influenza and chest infections had killed most of them.

The party set out on 30 January 1830, after being dropped at Recherche Bay by a schooner and a whaleboat, which would follow them up the coast carrying provisions. It included Robinson's second son, Charles, six convicts hoping for a pardon, and twelve Aborigines desperate to get away from jail or from 'civilisation' and its dangers. Among the Aborigines were Truganini, Woorraddy and his sons, Dray (who belonged to the Port Davey band) and Pagerly. Truganini was thrilled to be chosen to join the expedition. She idolised the energetic, forceful Yorkshireman, and was relieved to escape the petty rules and restrictions of 'civilised' life.

The job of Truganini and the other Aborigines on this expedition was to go on ahead, track down the 'wild' Aborigines and open negotiations. Then Robinson would promise the Aborigines that the government would look after them if they stopped fighting the white settlers. It was dangerous work: the Mission Aborigines were on other tribes' land and risked being speared for trespassing. Truganini was a fine linguist and quickly learned how to communicate with tribes who spoke a different language. Even so, it would sometimes take her hours to talk wary Aborigines into meeting Robinson.

Warlike Aborigines were not the only danger on this trek. Though Tasmania's south-west is breathtakingly beautiful, it is forbidding — no white people had attempted to hike through it before. Mountainous, with deep ravines, rushing rivers, enormous trees, dense bush, and very little game, it would daunt all but the most intrepid adventurers. Even a man as determined and energetic as Robinson would have failed without the skill and knowledge of his Aboriginal guides. The Aborigines went ahead and found native tracks, followed by the rest of the party in single file. Truganini had to hack through dense forests, crawl through underbrush on her hands and knees, and scramble over trees and rocky hillsides slippery with moss. She waded through rivers, descended steep cliffs and spent nights in deep ravines. Strong winds and driving rain soaked the tents and beds.

Though Robinson seemed to thrive on the hardship, this four-day trek was an ordeal for everyone else. Though the Aborigines were used to walking, they seldom trekked so far and in such difficult conditions. It was cold, wet and exhausting, and the food soon ran out — only two kangaroos were spotted, and there were no crayfish in the rivers.

Truganini, Dray and Pagerly survived on roasted yams until the party rendezvoused with the schooner at Louisa Bay. To make matters worse, they did not see a single Aborigine. The hundred or more Aboriginal shelters they came upon were all deserted.

At Port Davey, where they had to cross the mouth of the channel to continue north, they were faced with high winds and choppy seas. The Aborigines solved the problem by building a catamaran out of bark. Then, because none of the men could swim, the women had to ferry the whole party and their luggage across by holding onto the flimsy boat and swimming in front and behind. Truganini was a strong swimmer, and would be called on again and again to brave cold and dangerous rivers to ferry the others across.

Robinson being ferried across the Arthur River on a raft by the native women, from the diaries of George Augustus Robinson, 10 June 1830. Courtesy Mitchell Library, State Library of New South Wales.

At Spring River in the Bathurst Channel, they had to stop and fix the storm-damaged schooner before setting off north along the coast, heading for Launceston. It would take them six months to get there.

On the second leg of this expedition Robinson intended to make contact with the north-western and northern tribes. However, it wasn't till they were nearing Macquarie Harbour that they met any Aborigines. These were members of the Port Davey band, Dray's people. She, Truganini and Pagerly tried to talk them into joining the Mission, but failed. When the party left, Dray remained behind.

This trek turned into quite an ordeal. To add to the general discomfort, everybody caught an itchy skin disease. Robinson tried to cure his with an ointment made of gunpowder and urine; it didn't work. When they reached Macquarie Harbour, he sent Truganini, Woorraddy and Alexander McKay, the head convict, into the notoriously harsh penal settlement to get some ointment. The men dressed up in old scarlet army jackets, and marched in like tattered soldiers, with Truganini walking between them. The prisoners were delighted, and so was Truganini. She had a strong sense of mischief and fun, and loved to dance and sing. On this trek she even managed to persuade George Robinson to dance at the corroborees the Aborigines held when they struck camp after a long day.

On the north coast Robinson's expedition entered

the war zone. Here the north-west and north tribes were in constant violent conflict with shepherds from the Van Diemen's Land Company who had moved flocks into their hunting grounds. In 1830, in one of the most infamous incidents in Tasmanian history, shepherds had massacred thirty Pennemukeer people and thrown them over a cliff to avenge the wounding of a shepherd and the killing of a mob of sheep. In all, the north tribe had lost 140 of its members in battles with shepherds.

The north tribe had a great military asset, however — Tarerenorerer, the woman warrior. Walyer, as the sealers called her, had been abducted by Aborigines from Port Sorell, who then gave her to the sealers in exchange for dogs and flour. After some years she escaped from the sealers and became the leader of the Emu Bay people, whom she taught to use guns. Walyer would stand on a hill taunting the shepherds to come out of their huts and be speared by her warriors.

Not surprisingly, these tribes were suspicious of strangers. Sometimes Truganini would catch a glimpse of black warriors tracking them through the bush. One day Truganini and her group came upon a party of more than forty northern people at West Point. Frightened, the northern Aborigines jumped into the sea and swam to an island. Robinson ordered Truganini and Pagerly to swim out and talk them into returning. The women did not want to go, and their instincts were right. When they reached some rocks halfway out, a huge warrior on the island threatened them with a spear. They beat a hasty retreat to the beach.

One of the aims of this expedition was to rescue Aboriginal women stolen by the sealers. Skilled seal-hunters, the women were invaluable to the sealers, though they were often badly treated. When the Mission neared Hunter and Robbins Island, home of the sealers, Robinson took Truganini and Woorraddy across the channel to try to talk the women into joining them. This project was doomed: the Aboriginal women did not want to leave, and the sealers had no intention of letting them go. As a consolation prize, the sealers let Robinson take an Aboriginal man, Pevay or Tunnerminnerwate, whom they called Jack Napoleon. A noted warrior, Pevay became Robinson's right-hand man on the Friendly Mission, and ten years later was to play a fateful role in Truganini's life.

The troupe was now nearing Launceston and the end of the Mission. Despite a harsh winter and a shortage of provisions, they had contacted most of the south-west Aborigines, sighted some of the north-west people and avoided a confrontation with Walyer's guerilla band. Truganini herself had come through one of the most arduous treks in Australian history in perfect health. After a month of trudging through heavy snows in the Hampshire Hills, two of the Aborigines had fallen ill and Robinson's knee was abscessed, but Truganini's worst ailment was badly swollen legs from walking 56 kilometres in one day.

If Robinson had expected to be greeted as a conquering hero when he reached Launceston, he was disappointed. All the able-bodied men in the town were getting ready to go to war with the Aborigines. While he'd been in the bush, the war between the white farmers and the Oyster Bay and Big River Tribes had worsened. Determined to end the conflict, Governor Arthur had given orders for a military offensive against the Tasmanian Aborigines. Mounted soldiers and armed civilians formed themselves into a human dragnet, or 'Black Line', and set out to drive all the Aborigines into a trap at Forestier Peninsula in the south-east of the island. This misguided plan cost thirty thousand pounds — a massive fortune — and involved 2100 soldiers, convicts and civilians stretching over 190 kilometres. It netted one Aboriginal man and one boy, and killed two others. It was an abject failure: the Aborigines had no trouble evading the noisy, clumsy white men and melting into the landscape. However, it did mark the end of the worst hostilities between the races.

The failure of the Black Line created an opportunity for George Robinson. Though the Friendly Mission had brought in only one Aborigine so far, he was certain the rest would eventually surrender peacefully. He petitioned the government for money to extend the Mission. Believing the danger to the white settlers would not cease till all Aborigines were banished from the mainland, Governor Arthur agreed and set aside Flinders Island as an Aboriginal reserve.

Truganini spent the next four years trekking in the wilderness with Robinson. Now that they were actively trying to remove Aborigines from their lands, life had become much more dangerous for the Mission Aborigines. On a hunting trip in 1832, Truganini, Pagerly and Dray (who had returned from the bush) came upon a group of Arthur River Aborigines and brought them to meet Robinson. Though the strangers accepted beads, hankies, knives, plums and bread, the men were sullen and threatening. When one of the warriors stationed himself between Robinson and the river where the raft was tied up, everyone knew trouble was brewing. Sure enough, when the warriors went off hunting, their women told the Mission Aborigines that they were planning an attack.

On their return, the warriors began preparing their spears for action. They staged a corroboree that looked to Robinson like a rehearsal for a massacre, with himself and the Mission Aborigines as the victims. That night he pretended to sleep, but kept one eye on the chief of the Pieman River band, who sat at the end of his bed hardening his spears in the fire and straightening them with his teeth.

Truganini was sure they would all be murdered the next day. But when Woorraddy urged her to run away, she refused to leave Robinson. When dawn broke, the warriors lit fires and began working on their spears. When Woorraddy went to get his spear, it was missing. That was the last straw. Robinson packed his knapsack and told Pevay it was time to get out — the rest of the Aborigines could make up their own minds. But when Robinson made his move, the warriors surrounded them, spears poised. Truganini and her friends immediately fled into the bush, with Robinson at their heels. He quickly caught up with Truganini and stuck close. As he couldn't swim, he'd need her to push his raft across the river.

When they reached the river, Truganini wanted to hide, but Robinson hurried her along, knowing the trackers would find any hiding place. He insisted that they cross the river. Truganini protested that the warriors would be waiting for them by their raft. To Truganini's astonishment, Robinson found two logs, tied them together with his scarf and lay across them. Frightened for her life, Truganini pushed the makeshift raft out into the water and dog-paddled it across the river. They reached the other side safely, and

Truganini

walked back to camp. Robinson immediately saddled up his horse and rode back to the river, where he discovered that most of his people had crossed safely, bringing his tent and knapsacks. Four young women from the Arthur River band had come with them. Their terror over, the group set off for Cape Grim.

Many times on these expeditions Truganini was sorry she'd ever learned to swim. The rivers on the west coast were treacherous and icy. Once, leading some Pieman River people back to Macquarie Harbour in 1833, the Mission party found a cold, swiftly flowing river in their way. As usual, Truganini, Pagerly and Dray had to strip off and plunge into the freezing water, push the raft across and bring it back. They made the journey twenty-four times. That night Truganini suffered a seizure, probably from hypothermia, but soon recovered. On another trip she again saved Robinson's life by swimming out to his raft and towing it out of a dangerous rip.

The Friendly Mission ended in 1834, after six expeditions. In five years, Robinson and his troupe had trekked into the farthest corners of the island rounding up Aborigines. At the end of the Mission, only one Aboriginal family remained on the mainland. Their work done, Truganini and the other surviving members of the Mission were sent to Wybalenna on Flinders Island. Wybalenna was an early version of the concentration camp — a closed place where a group of people could be taken and isolated from the rest of society. The term later became synonymous with mistreatment, starvation and death. Though they were not starved, the Aborigines were forbidden to follow their tribal customs and beliefs, and denied their traditional way of life. Truganini had to work in the kitchen and the garden, and go to church and sing English hymns that meant nothing to her. The Aboriginal children had to attend schools in order to be 'civilised' so they could fit into white society.

The results were catastrophic. These Aborigines were the survivors of a long war. They had lost friends and relatives to violence and sickness, and had been driven from their homelands. Grief-stricken and forced into a confusing and alien way of life, they simply lost hope. Exposed to white food and white germs, they sickened and died. Of the 200 Aborigines sent to Wybalenna, 132 perished within four years.

In 1838 Truganini was plucked from this doomed settlement by her old mentor, George Robinson. He had been appointed Chief Protector of Aborigines at Port Phillip (now Victoria), and decided to organise a Friendly Mission to bring the Victorian Aborigines out of the bush. To do this, he would need the services of the experienced Van Diemen's Land Aborigines. Though the Aborigines around Port Phillip had fared better than the Tasmanians, they were in a sorry state. White expansion had forced some further out into the bush; the rest had settled in squalid camps on the outskirts of Melbourne. Sick, demoralised and ravaged by alcohol, some had turned to prostitution, or begging, to survive.

Desperate to escape from Wybalenna, Truganini looked forward to going adventuring with George Robinson again. Her hopes were soon dashed. Robinson became caught up in his new job, and had no time for his old friends or another Friendly Mission. Left to fend for themselves, several of the Aboriginal men went droving; others worked on properties belonging to Robinson's sons and other white settlers.

After thirteen years at Robinson's side helping him win fame and fortune, Truganini had been cast aside. Feeling betrayed and neglected, she grew increasingly angry. By now she had deserted Woorraddy, whom she'd never loved, and was lonely and bored. When Robinson left for a trip to the interior of Victoria in April 1840, she and her friends rebelled and began fraternising with the local Aborigines. Truganini ran away several times and was brought back. In a small settlement, the Aborigines' behaviour was noticed and gossiped about. A rumour spread through the colony that the Tasmanians were plotting with the local Aborigines to punish the whites who had stolen their lands. Farmers in the

Westernport and Mornington districts oiled their guns and prepared for the worst.

Robinson walked into this controversy on his return in August 1841. Angered by the trouble they were causing, he gave orders that the Tasmanian Aborigines be sent back to Flinders Island. When he heard about this, Pevay escaped into the bush. Truganini, who had no intention of going back to Wybalenna, crept out with three others — Matilda, Fanny and Robert Timmy — and set off to find Pevay.

The five Tasmanians lived off the land and occasionally stole sheep and cattle for food. Believing they had nothing to lose, they decided to take revenge for what had happened to their people in Tasmania and Victoria. They would rather go down fighting than go back to Van Diemen's Land to die of unhappiness. Elusive as shadows, they crept out of the bush and raided stations between Dandenong and Cape Paterson, stealing guns and supplies.

The campaign turned violent in October 1841, when the Aborigines swooped on the coal mine at Cape Paterson while the overseer was away. After ordering the women and children outside, they looted the miners' huts and set them on fire. When the overseer returned, shots were exchanged, and his son-in-law was wounded in the leg. Later, coming upon two white men and mistaking them for the overseer and his son-in-law, the Aborigines attacked.

In fact, the men were whalers who happened to be in the wrong place at the wrong time. The Aborigines shot one through the ear, and shot and bashed the other around the head. Leaving two dead bodies behind, they fled into the bush.

At this point Truganini feared they had gone too far — they had murdered two white men. She was right. The other men from the whalers' party went to the authorities. A search party was hastily organised. Led by Crown Commandant Powlett and Lieutenant Rawson, six police and six Aboriginal trackers set out to hunt down the Tasmanians. Hearing rumours that the renegades intended to fight to the death, landowners took fright and armed themselves to the teeth or took refuge in town.

For the first month, the Aborigines eluded their hunters easily. Frustrated, the government increased the search party to twenty-eight armed men. Then the Aborigines slipped up. On Saturday, 20 November, the white posse crept up on their camp and found them unprepared. The police opened fire, and hit Matilda, who ran into the bush with Pevay and Robert Timmy. The white men surrounded the camp and moved in. Tossing some blankets aside with their bayonets, they found Truganini and Fanny huddled underneath. They put guns to the women's heads and ordered them to call the others out of the bush. Knowing it was all over, Truganini obeyed. Matilda,

Robert Timmy and Pevay emerged, and were handcuffed and clapped in leg irons.

On 26 November the Tasmanian Aborigines arrived in Melbourne in chains under military escort. Horrified by what had happened to his old friends, and perhaps feeling guilty for abandoning them, George Robinson visited them in jail. When Truganini told him the jailers were predicting they'd all hang, he tried to calm her fears.

A jury was selected, and the Tasmanians were sent to trial for murder. George Robinson gave evidence on their behalf. He confirmed that he had known them for years and that they were of good character. He spoke particularly well of the warrior Pevay, and praised Truganini; he told the court how she had saved his life on the Friendly Mission. In an attempt to save the women, Robinson testified that custom in Van Diemen's Land required Aboriginal women to be subservient to their men, that the women had had no choice but to do as the men told them. Unaware that Truganini had been making her own decisions since girlhood, the jury believed him.

It took the jury only half an hour to decide the Tasmanians' fate. They found Pevay and Robert Timmy guilty of murder and acquitted Truganini, Fanny and Matilda. Despite a strong plea for mercy, the judge sentenced the men to hang. All Melbourne turned out for the hanging and acted as if it were a circus. Dressed in demeaning white costumes, Pevay and Robert Timmy were dragged out in front of about 5000 gawking spectators. It was a dreadful death: the convict hangman bungled the execution, and the men strangled slowly. The sight of two human beings struggling on the end of the rope horrified and chastened the crowd. Their festive mood darkened and they hissed and jeered at the executioner.

Six months later, five Tasmanian Aborigines were repatriated to Flinders Island. Six others had died on the Australian mainland, and two had stayed on. Woorraddy died on the voyage from Port Phillip.

Back at Wybalenna, Truganini began absconding from the settlement and spending time with sealers. Regarding her as a bad influence on the other young women, Superintendent Henry Jeanneret — a hard, unbending man — forced her into an unofficial 'marriage' with Mannapackername ('Big Jemmy'), a member of the Big River Tribe. Truganini spent five years at Wybalenna, after which the government decided to shut it down. By then there were only forty-six Aborigines still alive. The survivors were shipped to Oyster Cove, 40 kilometres south of Hobart. From there Truganini could see her birthplace across the channel — so near and yet so far.

Truganini's life at Oyster Cove was miserable. Mannapackername died there, leaving her widowed for the second time. The other Aborigines shunned

Australian Heroines

Detail from *Aborigines and settlers at Oyster Cove in 1847*, pencil drawing by Annie Benbow c. 1900. Collection Tasmanian Art Gallery & Museum.

her. They knew about her exploits on the Friendly Mission and blamed her for helping bring her fellow Aborigines in to Flinders Island, where so many of them died.

What had induced Truganini to join the Friendly Mission and help Robinson talk her people into surrendering? Some people believe that she was in love with Robinson and did it for him. Others think she enjoyed the power. But it's just as likely that she realised the Tasmanians were doomed and believed that bringing them out of the bush would save the few that were left. According to Truganini herself, she'd realised that Aboriginal resistance was futile as a teenager on her first visit to Hobart. 'It was no use my people trying to kill all the white people now, there were so many of them always coming in big boats,' she said. She had helped George Robinson, she explained, because he was not like the other white men and offered the Aborigines protection from violence. In Truganini's defence, she could not have foreseen that they would be interned on an island where they would die of illness and despair.

In 1851 Robinson decided to return to England. He visited his old friends at Oyster Cove on his way. He and Truganini reminisced about their great adventures. By then, there were only thirty adults still alive, and only four Aboriginal children in the Queen's Orphan School. Oyster Cove was cold and damp, and many died from chest infections. Alcohol brought in by whites killed others. Six years later, the population had fallen to five men and ten women, and no babies were being born.

At Oyster Cove Truganini married her third husband, William Lanney, an Aboriginal whaler. This time Truganini had fallen in love, and was possessive of her much younger husband. In 1867 dysentery swept through Oyster Cove, killing off two of the last three Aboriginal women. Truganini stayed on with her husband and Mary-Anne, who was part-Aboriginal. William Lanney died in 1869, aged only 34. Truganini was alone, the last tribal Aborigine in mainland Tasmania.

Taking pity on her, John Dandridge, Superintendent of the Oyster Cove Aboriginal Station, moved her in with his family. In her old age, she made many trips back to Bruny Island to camp in the bush. Surrounded by the ghosts of the Nuenonne, Truganini remembered her childhood; shinnying up tall trees chasing possums, diving for crayfish, hunting mutton-bird, creeping up to swans' nests to steal eggs. Her back against a tree, gazing out over the channel, she day-dreamed about her great adventures with George Robinson on the Friendly Mission — bashing through almost impenetrable bush, swimming raging torrents with Dray, dancing and singing around the camp-fire after a hard day's trek, facing down hostile Aboriginal warriors. And she would remember her special friendship with the remarkable Yorkshireman with the funny hat.

In 1873 Dandridge moved his household to Hobart, to 115 Macquarie Street. After his death, his widow continued to care for Truganini, who was now an old woman. Legends sprang up about the stout little figure in the red turban, and she became known as the 'Queen' of her race and 'the last Tasmanian'. But Truganini was not the last Tasmanian — members of her race had survived on islands in Bass Strait, particularly Cape Barren Island where the sealers' women had settled. In the 1970s their descendents identified themselves as Aborigines.

Truganini died in May 1876 at the age of 64. During her lifetime, she had seen the white men move in, overrun the tribal hunting grounds and change her homeland forever, bringing in strange animals, cutting down trees and building farms and towns. She had witnessed the destruction of a way of life that had lasted over 35 000 years.

The War Against the First Tasmanians

When Abel Jantzen Tasman 'discovered' Van Diemen's Land in 1642, it was home to between five and seven thousand Aborigines who had migrated from the Australian mainland over a land bridge about thirty-six thousand years before. Ten thousand years later the seas rose and severed the land link, cutting them off from the mainland and isolating their culture.

Truganini's tribe first came into contact with white people in 1773 when Captain James Cook's ships, the *Resolution* and the *Discovery*, anchored at Adventure Bay on Bruny Island. He was followed by the French explorers D'Entrecasteaux, Labillardière and Baudin between 1793 and 1801.

These visitors regarded the natives of Van Diemen's Land as hopelessly primitive — a 'stone age' people. The Aborigines had no metal, dogs, boomerangs or axes with ground edges. They did not build permanent houses, but slept under the stars or in caves on the sea-shore in summer, and took shelter in wind-breaks made of tree branches in cold weather. They went naked except in the depths of winter, when they covered their shoulders and waists with kangaroo skins. To ward off the cold and damp, they rubbed a pungent mixture of animal grease and ash onto their bodies. Both men and women wore tribal scars. The women shaved their heads with shells or flints, while the men wore dreadlocks like lambs' tails hardened with red ochre and grease. Small groups moved around their territory following traditional hunting routes and carrying a smouldering stick to make fires.

Believing the white men were their ancestors come back to life, the Aborigines were at first friendly towards the newcomers, and curious. But when sealers, kangaroo hunters and escaped convicts from New South Wales arrived and began plundering their hunting grounds and stealing their women, the Aborigines retaliated. They had no weapons against the exotic diseases brought in by the foreigners, however, and many died from illnesses such as colds and measles.

When the British arrived and built convict settlements on the Derwent and Tamar rivers in 1803, it was the beginning of the end for traditional Aboriginal society in Van Diemen's Land. After some violent confrontations, the Governor armed the convicts, and many Aborigines were injured or killed. Worse was to come. During the 1820s immigrants from Britain began to flood in, attracted by the promise of free land. They moved out into the open forests and grasslands between Hobart in the south and Launceston in the north, building homesteads, fencing off Aboriginal hunting grounds, and introducing sheep and cattle. Faced with starvation, the Aborigines stole stock and food. The settlers defended their property, often with guns, and the Aborigines fought back. In 1830 this conflict escalated into a full-scale war. By 1831, 175 Europeans had been killed and 200 wounded: Aboriginal casualties were probably higher. The war was, to all intents and purposes, over by 1834, when George Augustus Robinson brought in the last of the 'wild' Aborigines from beyond the white frontier.

What guns and disease had begun, displacement from tribal lands and internment on Flinders Island ended. Truganini's death in 1876, and that of a woman called Suke in 1888, saw the last tribal Tasmanian Aborigines pass into history. Descendants of Aboriginal women and white sealers survived in sealers' camps on islands in Bass Strait, however, and they proudly identified themselves as Aborigines in the 1970s, a century after Truganini's death.

The Battle for the Bones

In the nineteenth century scientists would go to extraordinary lengths to get hold of the bodies of tribal Aborigines, purportedly for research. In life, Truganini had dreaded ending up like her third husband, William Lanney. Believing Lanney was one of the last tribal Tasmanians, when in fact he was part New South Wales Aborigine, scientists had stolen and dismembered his body and extracted his skeleton. All Truganini's worst fears came true. As the last tribal Tasmanian Aborigine, she was regarded as a priceless specimen, and after her death a fierce battle broke out over her remains.

To foil the body snatchers, Truganini's friends buried her secretly within the walls of the Cascades Penitentiary. But people talked. A few days after her death Truganini's body was dug up and boiled down to the skeleton, which was then spirited off to the Tasmanian Museum, where her bones were stored in an apple box. In the 1890s the bones were almost thrown out by mistake.

Despite promises to the contrary, the museum put Truganini's skeleton on display in 1904. It stayed there, gawked at by generations of school children, till 1950, when a campaign was launched to give Truganini's remains a decent burial. Scientists resisted because the skeleton was the only existing specimen of a tribal Tasmanian Aborigine. The Tasmanian government caved in to pressure, and moved Truganini's skeleton to a specially designed section of the museum. In 1965, however, it was quietly placed in a vault.

When the Aboriginal rights movement began in the early 1970s, Truganini's skeleton became the centre of a major political and racial controversy. The Aborigines won, and in 1976 her remains were cremated. On 1 May, just seven days short of the centenary of her death, Truganini's ashes were scattered in the D'Entrecasteaux Channel. She had gone home.

Aborigines are still battling to recover the bones and skulls of their ancestors from museums and universities in Australia and Europe.

Barbara Crawford Thompson

Shipwrecked

HMS Rattlesnake *and* Bramble, *the ships that rescued Barbara Thompson*, drawn by Owen Stanley in 1848. Courtesy Mitchell Library, State Library of New South Wales.

On 16 October 1849, the crew of a British warship on its way back from New Guinea went ashore near the tip of Cape York to look for fresh water. To their astonishment they found Barbara Thompson, a white woman who'd been living with a tribe of Torres Strait Islanders for five years.

Barbara Crawford was born in Aberdeen, Scotland in about 1826, and migrated to New South Wales with her parents at the age of eight. The Crawfords settled in Kent Street in The Rocks, on Sydney Harbour. The Rocks was a wild place. Crowded, noisy and lively, it was populated largely by English and Irish convicts who'd won their tickets of leave.

A tinsmith, Barbara's father found work at the wharves, and for a while the family prospered. But when he lost his job because of his drinking, the Crawfords fell on hard times, and he turned to petty theft. Barbara desperately wanted to get away. She was sick of the fights over money and the endless scrimping and saving. Her big chance came shortly before her fifteenth birthday. She fell in love with a confident, ambitious young seaman, William Thompson, who convinced her to run away with him to Moreton Bay. Over a thousand kilometres to the north, Moreton Bay was the new frontier. Fortunes could be made there by those prepared to take a risk.

Moreton Bay had a grim past as a dumping ground for the colony's worst convicts. Under cruel commanders like Captain Patrick Logan, the convicts had been worked like slaves, and whipped for breaking the rules. Only recently made a free settlement, Brisbane, the town which had sprung up on the river, still had many terrible reminders of those days. The centre of the town was dominated by a treadmill, on which the convicts had been forced to march endlessly, milling wheat. The General Post Office had once been a jail for female convicts, many of whom had been put to work building roads. The police force consisted of former convicts. Fifteen years later, Brisbane would become the capital of a new state, Queensland.

With its broad river, mountain views and lush tropical vegetation, Brisbane was attractive after the crowded slums of The Rocks. But Barbara found the suffocating, sticky heat exhausting, and was kept awake at night by swarms of mosquitoes from the mangrove swamps around the bay. The afternoon storms that brought blissful cool also turned narrow dirt roads into quagmires. But for a young couple, Moreton Bay was different, exciting — an adventure. Barbara wrote to her father telling him that she was with William and was safe in Brisbane. She was hurt when he didn't answer; in fact, he was in jail for receiving stolen goods, and didn't ever see the letter.

William, a clever, practical man, could have made his name as an adventurer. Ludwig Leichhardt, the German explorer, tried to recruit him for his epic 5000-kilometre trek to Port Essington on Australia's northern coast, but William turned him down. Although he did indeed plan to try his luck in Port Essington, he intended to sail there. In a tavern in Brisbane, he'd met an old sailor who had survived a shipwreck on the Bampton Shoal in Torres Strait, off Cape York. The seaman was looking for a partner to help him salvage the valuable whale oil on the wrecked ship.

When William described the venture to Barbara, she was dubious at first. It was a long way to Port Essington, she argued, and they would be completely on their own. Along the coast north of Brisbane there were no white settlements where they could buy provisions, and if they went ashore, they could be attacked by Aborigines. As witnessed by the wreck of the whaler, Torres Strait was dangerous, full of submerged reefs. William talked her around. If they managed to salvage the wreck, they would arrive in Port Essington with a valuable commodity to sell. Their future would be secure. Somehow he raised the money to buy the *America*, a ten-ton cutter, and fitted it out himself for the long voyage. Then he recruited a crew.

In August 1844, Leichhardt set out for the Darling Downs to begin his expedition. The following month, the *America* — with William, Barbara, the old salt and two other seamen aboard — sailed north from Moreton Bay. After a promising start, the voyage soon turned into an ordeal. The crew squabbled, and they ran out of food and had to live on fish and shellfish. But their troubles had only just begun. The ship's dinghy, carrying William, the two sailors and a load of firewood, overturned and sank. The two sailors drowned, and William survived only because he was a strong swimmer.

When the *America* finally reached Torres Strait, the old seaman couldn't find the wreck. William was angry, believing that the man had lied to him. Barbara became frightened and anxious. All their high hopes had ended in disappointment. Worse was to come. The wet season had begun and they were hit with two weeks of bad weather. Looking for shelter, William anchored the *America* off Horn Island on the Barrier Reef. They survived the night, but the next morning the tide went out, leaving the cutter stranded on a reef. The situation was bad, but not yet desperate. They'd seen a canoe full of Torres Strait Islanders fishing for

Australian Heroines

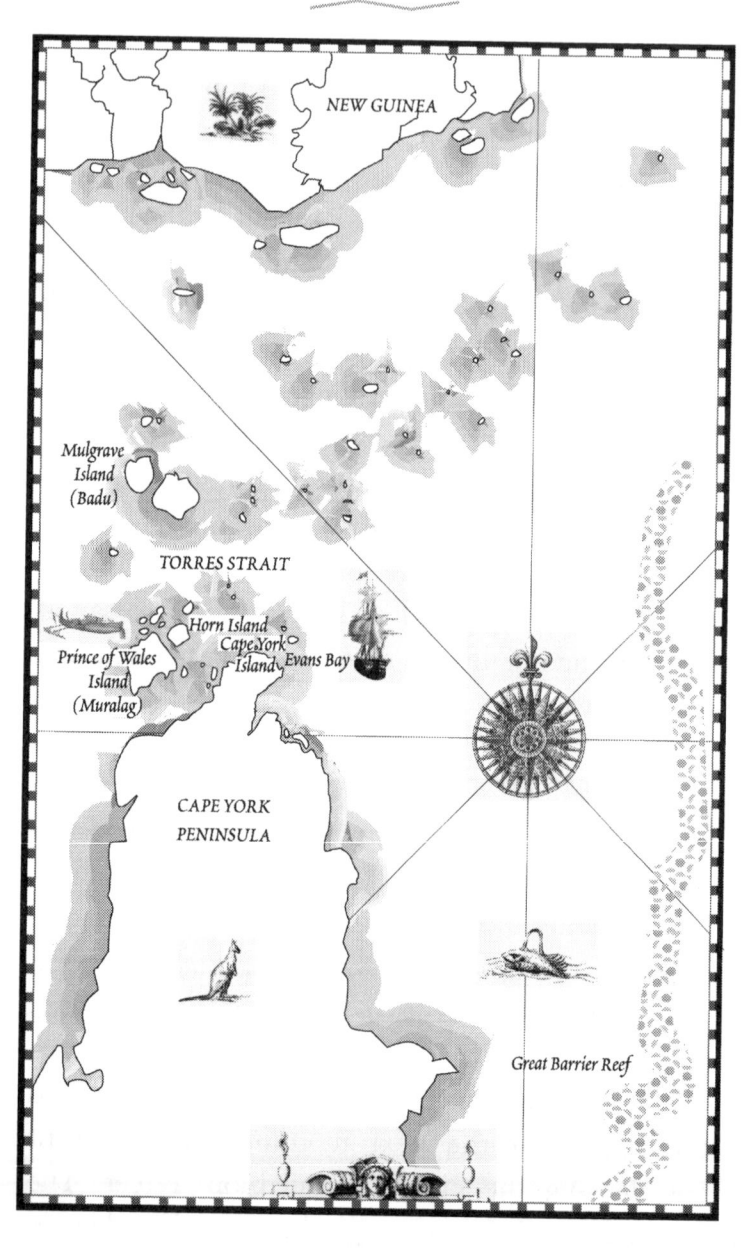

Map showing the place where Barbara Thompson was shipwrecked; where she lived with the Torres Strait Islanders for five years; and where she was rescued. Map drawn by Stanish Graphics.

turtles on the reef, so they knew there had to be people living nearby.

Then a sudden squall blew up, broadsiding the cutter with huge waves and driving winds. The ship began to break up beneath them. With the dinghy long gone, there was no choice but to swim for shore to look for help. But Barbara could not swim. Terrified that she would die alone, she begged William not to leave her. He tried to calm her down. If they stayed, they'd all die, he reasoned. This way there was a chance he could get help before the wreck sank.

Barbara and William embraced. With one last look William dived into the water, followed by the old sailor. Barbara watched as they swam away, struggling in the churning sea. Then the old man went down. Barbara held her breath. William would be fine, she told herself. He was a good swimmer. But the weeks of semi-starvation had weakened him. Barbara's young husband disappeared beneath the waves. He didn't come up again. Sobbing, alone in the middle of raging seas, Barbara clung to the battered boat. Unless a miracle happened, she was finished. Even if the boat remained afloat, she'd soon die of thirst in the pitiless tropical heat.

Then the storm began to die down, and she heard a human voice. Wondering if she'd imagined it, she scanned the seas. It was the Torres Strait Islanders they'd seen hunting turtles. The fishermen had taken refuge inside the reef when the storm struck and had ridden it out. They rowed up and called out to Barbara. Soon, strong brown arms were around her and she was taken off the boat and placed in the canoe.

Barbara didn't know what to feel. She was grateful to have been saved from drowning, but what would happen to her now? Surreptitiously, she eyed the men. She'd heard stories about the wild tribes of Aborigines who inhabited Cape York. Some were friendly, but others reacted violently when white people invaded their territory. She tried to stay calm and keep her wits about her. Then the canoe neared a substantial island. On the white man's maps it was called Prince of Wales Island, but to its traditional owners, the Kaurareg, it was known as Muralag.

Barbara felt a new spurt of fear as she caught sight of some native huts, but when they reached land, the men did not harm her. Instead, they helped her ashore and covered her with dry pandanus mats to keep her warm. One of them boiled up some turtle soup and gave it to her in a big shell. Her spirits began to revive. They wouldn't be feeding her, surely, if they intended to kill her.

News of the turtle hunters' strange catch spread quickly. A large group of natives ran down to the beach. As her saviours — Tomagugu, Alikia and Boroto — retold the story of the shipwreck and the rescue, the natives stared at Barbara, discussed her appearance, and fingered her hair and clothes. Trembling, she searched the curious faces for a clue to her fate. It was settled when Peaqui, one of the tribal elders, decided that Barbara was the ghost (*marki*) of his dead daughter, Giom, come back to them. Barbara was lucky. If another tribe had found her, she could easily have been killed. So Barbara became Giom, or Gioma, and was accepted into the tribe.

For a time, Barbara was too stunned by the shipwreck and death of her husband to take in what was happening. Then the reality hit her. Yes, she was lucky to be alive, but what sort of life would it be? At 17, she was stranded on an isolated island, at the mercy of people she did not understand, separated from her home, her family and her civilisation. Overcome by homesickness and grief, she often cried herself to sleep.

But Barbara was a strong, sensible girl. Gradually she tried to adapt to her new surroundings. Physically, it was a hard life. Although the largest of the western Torres Strait Islands — about 320 kilometres in circumference — Prince of Wales Island was no tropical paradise. Part of the coastline had sandy beaches and streams, but the interior was hilly and rugged, with scrubby undergrowth. There was a lake on the island, but it was surrounded by barren country.

The food supply was poor: unlike more fertile

islands, Muralag had no animals, and grew no coconuts or bananas. As a result, the tribe was nomadic, moving between the islands in the Muralag group and the mainland to trade and to harvest yams. To survive, the Kaurareg relied on fishing — spearing turtles and dugong, trapping fish at the mouths of creeks, collecting shellfish — and digging up yams. To find yams and to collect water, the women had to walk miles into the stony hills. During the wet season, when the seas were too rough to fish, they lived mainly on edible mangroves which grew in two creeks at the south-east corner of the island.

Barbara lived with a kindly woman called Urdzanna and her husband Gunage. In the summer, the tribe camped in the open; in the winter, they sheltered in humpies built from bamboo and tea-tree bark. Fires kept them warm. Unused to sleeping beside an unguarded fire, Barbara rolled into the embers and burned herself, scarring her leg and side, and almost losing an eye. But the Kaurareg did their best to protect their Gioma. When they realised she wasn't strong enough to make the foraging treks into the hills, they let her stay at home with the old women to mind the children.

Barbara quickly picked up the tribal language. At first she used to sing Scottish ballads to herself at night so she would not forget her own language, but gradually her English slipped away and she began to think in Kaurareg. Culturally, it was a huge transition for a Scottish Presbyterian lass. The Kaurareg laughed when she told them there was only one God: they had many. The men went naked, and the women wore only grass skirts. When Barbara's clothes eventually fell to pieces, she wore the same. Babies born to unmarried mothers were taken away and smothered. Girls were married as young as 10 or 11 years of age, and men could have several wives. But by far the most frightening custom was head-hunting.

The tribes in Torres Strait were warlike. Though some got along, others were sworn enemies. The Kaurareg tribe's worst enemy was the Badulaig tribe from Mulgrave Island. In battles with the Badu, men were often killed and women abducted. The Kaurareg also fought with the mainland Aborigines, and when the Gumakudin killed Boroto's father, Kaurareg warriors raided them and returned with the heads of the killers. Barbara watched in horror as the men cooked and ate the heads and then held a victory corroboree.

As a white woman, Barbara was in particular danger. When the Badu heard she was on Muralag, they came to investigate. They decided she'd make a good wife for Weenie, who was probably a shipwrecked Indonesian sailor they'd adopted. Later they sent a party of sixteen canoes to kidnap her. Fortunately Barbara had enough warning to run away and hide in the hills till the Badu gave up and left. It took her weeks to get over the terror.

Although the Kaurareg treated her well — Urdzanna was good to her, and Boroto, Alikia and Tomagugu became her protectors — Barbara never became reconciled to spending the rest of her life on Muralag. Every now and then, news would filter through that would set her heart racing and raise her hopes. From smoke signals — the natives' bush telegraph — she knew that white men were beginning to open up Cape York, and English ships often sailed past on their way to China. Ships' crews occasionally came ashore at Cape York, but the Kaurareg never let them see Barbara. They were afraid they'd be shot for kidnapping a white woman.

Once, a ship anchored close to the island. Frantic, Barbara tried to attract the attention of the sailors on board. But though she cooeed loudly, they took no notice. Instead they took up the anchor and slowly moved away. Unable to bear the disappointment, Barbara crept away to a water-hole and howled. Thinking she was lost, the Kaurareg called out to her for hours, but she ignored them. Only the coming of night forced her back to the camp.

In 1846, when Barbara had been living on Muralag for two years, an old 28-gun British Navy vessel called the HMS *Rattlesnake* sailed from England on an expedition to survey the coasts of

Australia and New Guinea. Cramped, unventilated and crowded with 180 officers and men — and innumerable vermin — the frigate was commanded by Captain Owen Stanley.

Also on board were two Englishmen, Oswald Brierly and Thomas Huxley. An artist, navigator and rigger, Brierly had already voyaged around the world and had jumped at the chance of this journey to escape from managing an isolated whaling station (now Eden) at Twofold Bay. At 21, Thomas Huxley was doing a tour of duty as Assistant Surgeon because he was too young to sit for the examination of the Royal College of Surgeons which would license him to practise. The expedition had its own naturalist, John MacGillivray, a 27-year-old Scot, but the ambitious Huxley didn't let that stand in his way. Hoping this voyage would make his name as a biologist back home, he set up his own microscope in a corner of the chart room and started catching and examining sea creatures and writing up his findings.

On 8 May 1849, the *Rattlesnake* set sail from Sydney for New Guinea. Five months later, after completing the survey mission, the ship began its return journey down the coast of Cape York. Then fate put Barbara Thompson and the HMS *Rattlesnake* on a collision course. Noticing that some of the Kaurareg men were smoking tobacco, Barbara asked them where they'd got it. From a ship moored at

Evans Bay, over at Cape York, said her friend Tomagugu. A ship at Cape York! After five years in exile, this could be her chance to escape ... Barbara became so obsessed with the idea of reaching the ship that she couldn't eat. Trying to hide her anxiety from the tribe, she watched and waited.

Finally, the tribe decided to make an expedition to the ship to barter for more white man's goods. Barbara begged Urdzanna and Gunage to take her along. Desperation made her persuasive. She managed to convince them she wouldn't run away — all she wanted was medicine for her sore nose and her injured knee. Gunage gave in and said she could go in a canoe with Aburda, one of the old women.

Two days later, four canoes set off from Muralag, arriving at Cape York at nightfall. The local Aborigines welcomed them, showing off the knives, shirts and biscuits they'd traded with the sailors. They directed the Kaurareg to Wamalug (Cape York Island), which had plenty of water and a good beach. As the tribe dined on turtle and the men made themselves dizzy and sick smoking tobacco, Barbara plotted her escape. As soon as the men went fishing the next day, she went round to the eastern side of the island and gazed longingly at the ship across the water. Aburda asked if the white men would keep Barbara. Barbara said no, she was too black for them.

Barbara was in a quandary. If she pushed too hard,

the tribe would suspect she intended to defect; if she didn't push hard enough, they might 'forget' to take her. And sure enough, when a group set out for Cape York later that day, they left her behind. Desolate, she went to her perch, gazed at the ship and cried. Finally Aburda took pity and said she could go across the next day.

Up with the dawn, Barbara waited in a stew of frustration. In the afternoon, Aburda came back from the eastern side of the island calling out 'Giom! Come and look!' She'd seen some white men across on the headland shooting birds. The men rushed down to their canoes and set off towards them. Tomagugu's wife, Sibi, invited her to come with a group of Cape York Aborigines. Terrified of being left behind again, Barbara ran after them, leaving her grass skirt and basket behind. But when she waded out to get into the canoe, the Aborigines rowed off. Dragged out of her depth, Barbara clung on fiercely. Finally, one of the old men and his wife took pity and pulled her into the canoe.

The first party of Torres Strait Islanders to disembark discovered white men washing their clothes at the water-holes near Evans Bay. By the time Barbara's canoe arrived, a group of natives and curious sailors were waiting on the beach. Barbara was last off the canoe. What the sailors saw was a dark-skinned, dirty, naked native woman with matted

A *Kaurareg canoe*, sketched by Oswald Brierly. Courtesy Mitchell Library, State Library of New South Wales.

hair and a scarred body. Then she began to speak to them in halting English. Astonished, the sailors suddenly realised this was a white woman. Tomagugu tried to tell them how he'd rescued Barbara, but she stopped him. 'Friend, hold your tongue,' she said. 'I know what they're saying.'

When the sailors questioned her, Barbara told them she was from Muralag, and that Tomagugu was the 'brother' who'd saved her life. But after five years, her English had become rusty and she often had to stop and think how to phrase her thoughts. 'I forget English since I saw my country,' she explained. 'I sing the song I knew when I lay down at night, to remember it.'

One of the sailors called over a Scotsman called Scott. Barbara found him much easier to understand. Scott offered her food, and asked if the Torres Strait Islanders would release her to the men at the waterhole. When Tomagugu agreed, one of the men gave Barbara a biscuit and pulled off his shirt to cover her nakedness. Tomagugu immediately cadged the shirt for his little boy. Then Scott and Sergeant Mew, one of the officers, took Barbara off into the bush, gently washed her, combed her hair and dressed her in two shirts — one as a blouse, one as a skirt. Later, Barbara explained to Oswald Brierly, the ship's artist, how she'd felt: 'I was so ashamed when I got to the washing place that I did not notice what men were there. But this Scott was a friend of all of them. He took hold of me so bravelike. As I went along I could hardly speak for crying.'

Returning from a shooting expedition, Oswald Brierly and a fellow officer found a young woman, surrounded by a group of natives and sailors, eating from a tin plate. She was dressed in an odd costume made from sailors' shirts, and had a scarred face and red, inflamed eyes. As the officers approached, three Kaurareg warriors — Barbara's 'brothers' — drew into a tight, defensive circle around her.

Noticing that the natives were becoming anxious, the Englishmen realised they had to get her aboard the ship quickly. There could be trouble if the Kaura-reg discovered Giom was leaving them for good. To allay their suspicions, Barbara told them she was going on board the ship to see the white women. She invited Gunage, Urdzanna's husband, to go with her. When he refused, Alikia, Boroto and Tomagugu went instead.

Flanked by her rescuers, black and white, Barbara was carried down to a dinghy and rowed out to the *Rattlesnake*. When the Captain questioned Barbara, asking if she wanted to return to Sydney with the ship, she said simply: 'I am a Christian.' When the cook gave her a slice of apple pie, she said: 'I never thought of tasting the likes of this again.' While the ship lay at Cape York, some of the tribe anchored their canoes under Barbara's porthole and tried to convince her to stay. She refused. Neither would she return to their camp on the beach, fearing they might kill her now that they knew she wanted to go home.

To the scientists John MacGillivray and Thomas Huxley, Barbara was a Godsend. They quickly discovered that she had learned a great deal about plants and fish from the Torres Strait Islanders. Though she could not read or write, Barbara struck everyone on the ship as truthful, sincere, intelligent and highly observant. But it was the artist, Oswald Brierly, we can thank for the details of this saga. Fascinated by

Barbara Crawford Thompson

Aboriginal customs and language, he questioned Barbara at length and recorded her observations in his diary.

Unfortunately, nobody on board — including Brierly, the ship's artist — drew Barbara, so we have no record of what she looked like. Perhaps she was self-conscious about her damaged eye. All we know is that she was about 23, darkly tanned, and in Huxley's view, 'not bad looking'. When she was rescued, she had infected eyes and a sore knee, but these soon cleared up with medical treatment. The crew found some bolts of fabric, and Barbara passed the time sewing, making herself two gowns to wear.

The *Rattlesnake* reached Sydney with its curious cargo on 5 February 1850. The *Sydney Morning Herald* ran Barbara's extraordinary story the next day, but she quickly dropped from sight. It was only when John MacGillivray's account of the voyage of the *Rattlesnake* was published in 1852 that interest in her revived.

In 1977, some of Barbara Thompson's descendants were discovered living in Sydney. They revealed that Barbara had married twice after her rescue — once in 1851 to James Adams, with whom she had a daughter, Susan; and then to John William Simpson in 1876. Barbara lived for almost a century, dying in the 1920s, obviously none the worse for her extraordinary adventure among the Torres Strait Islanders.

And what of her rescuers?

Australian Heroines

Oswald Brierly was 32 when he met Barbara Thompson in 1949. He continued his voyaging and painting, becoming a famous marine painter and a favourite of the British royal family, who knighted him. He died in 1894 at the age of 77. His diaries are in the Mitchell Library in Sydney, and were published in David Moore's book, *Aborigines and Islanders at Cape York*. Without them, we would know very little about Barbara Thompson's story, and even less about the Kaurareg and their way of life.

Thomas Huxley was right in believing the voyage of the *Rattlesnake* would make his name as a biologist. His research on the ship led to his election to the prestigious Royal Society at 25 and won him a Royal Medal. He went on to revolutionise the teaching of biology, becoming one of the most influential scientists of the nineteenth century.

Born in Aberdeen, like Barbara, and a trained physician, **John MacGillivray** sailed to South America as a ship's naturalist after the Cape York voyage. In 1852 he published an acclaimed account of the voyage of the HMS *Rattlesnake*. He spent the rest of his life travelling among the islands off Australia collecting specimens and studying the Aborigines. His health broken, he died at the age of 45 in 1867.

Two months after the *Rattlesnake*'s return to Sydney, **Captain Owen Stanley** died of epilepsy at the age of 39. His name lives on in the Owen Stanley

Range in New Guinea. A collection of his drawings is housed in the Mitchell Library in Sydney.

As a tribe, **the Kaurareg** survived Barbara's departure by only twenty years. Once Cape York was explored and a white settlement established at Somerset in 1863, tribal life on the Torres Strait Islands was doomed. Missionaries found Barbara's adopted 'father', Peaqui, and other friends still alive on Prince of Wales Island in 1867, but two years later they were gone. Blamed for capturing a small vessel in Torres Strait and massacring the captain, his wife and son, and the ship's crew, the Kaurareg were pursued relentlessly by the white police. The warriors fought back, but spears were no match for guns. Those who survived left the island and scattered. It was discovered, too late, that a tribe from Mt Ernest Island had killed the seamen and that the captain's wife and son were alive in Melbourne.

By the end of the century, it was almost impossible to find any Kaurareg who remembered the old ways. Without Barbara Thompson's testament, the tribe would have vanished from history, leaving nothing but a few middens and some cave paintings. It was not only the Kaurareg who disappeared. By the end of the century, traditional life in Western Torres Strait had been wiped out by white expansion, Christian missionaries and the establishment of a government post at Thursday Island.

Sarah White Musgrave

Sarah of the South-west Plains

Sarah White Musgrave aged 102 with her great-great-granddaughter, Borise Antonia Isackson, in 1936. Photo courtesy Borise Isackson Hawtin.

Sarah White Musgrave

Sarah White was born in 1834, the first white child on the plains of south-west New South Wales, now the Young district. She survived floods and droughts and raids by bushrangers, and lived through a gold rush on her family's land.

Sarah's story really begins with her uncle, James White, who pioneered what is now the Young district in New South Wales. In 1826, he set off alone with a saddle-horse and a pack-horse to look for land beyond the frontier of white settlement. As the fertile pastures beyond the Blue Mountains had already been taken up, he travelled west to Parramatta, then turned south and rode past Camden, Picton and Goulburn. At Goulburn, he turned west. It was a gruelling and dangerous journey. Once he left the settled areas, James was at the mercy of the weather, the terrain and chance. In the bush, a fall from a horse or even a chill could prove fatal, and hostile Aborigines were a constant threat.

But James White was tough and lucky. Unscathed, he pushed his way further west than any other white man had ever gone. He saw smoke from camp fires, but met no Aborigines. After ten months and 400 kilometres, saddle-sore and weary, James found what he had been looking for — fertile grasslands as far as the eye could see, with a creek running through. He pitched camp and lit a fire. But unknown to him, he was being tracked by a band of Wiradjuri warriors. Looking up from his damper and tea one night, James was startled to see a tall warrior standing nearby, watching him, but he relaxed slightly when he noticed the Aborigine's spear was pointing down at the ground, not at him. James gestured to the man to sit down. When he realised the white man was not going to harm him, the Aborigine made a signal and several other warriors appeared out of the dark.

Somehow, the Englishman and the Wiradjuri tribesman managed to communicate. The warrior, who appeared to be a leader or chief, was called Cobborn and the land they were sitting on was Burrowmunditroy. But when Cobborn realised James White wanted to occupy Burrowmunditroy, he shook his head angrily. James stood up, went to his packhorse and reached into his saddle-bag. Alarmed, the Aborigines raised their spears, but lowered them when they realised it was not a weapon he was taking out of his saddle-bag, but foodstuffs, matches and tomahawks. With these peace offerings, James White began a friendship with Cobborn that would last till the white man's death in 1865.

In return for the gifts, Cobborn agreed to let James White occupy Burrowmunditroy and promised that the Wiradjuri would not attack him. On the strength of this agreement, James returned to Sydney, paid the government ten pounds for the right to settle on 259 square kilometres of land, and bought two bullock teams, sheep, cattle, horses, pigs and stores to stock his new property. He hired stockmen, loaded drays with household goods and tools, and set off on the long journey back to Burrowmunditroy. He was away ten months, and returned a squatter.

In Sydney James White had bought a crescent-shaped brass plate on a neck chain and had the name Cobborn Jackie inscribed on it. He presented this to Cobborn and declared him chief of Burrowmunditroy. To return the favour, the Aborigines held a celebratory corroboree that lasted ten days and Cobborn led James 8 kilometres south, through thick bush, to a site beside a deep, permanent creek. Recognising prime real estate when he saw it, James White immediately took possession. He had his station hands chop a road through and bring in the bullocks and supplies. Then they built a slab house, a dairy, men's quarters and other outhouses. James White named the station Burrangong.

In 1834 James's brother John joined him at Burrangong, bringing his new wife, Eliza Waterworth. In May that year, Eliza gave birth to Sarah, the first white child born on the south-west plains. The following year, the Whites had another daughter, whom they named Eliza.

Life on a property was not for the squeamish. One of Sarah's first memories was watching the station hands slaughtering emus. The men herded the birds into a yard, chopped off their heads, tanned their hides to make mats and boiled the carcasses down to make ointment for rheumatism. Nothing was wasted in the bush. Only the hardy survived on the frontier. Women sometimes died in childbirth. People were bitten by snakes; injured or killed by Aborigines; fell from horses and perished in the bush — Sarah's tutor almost died once when he got lost. As there were no doctors or hospitals, the pioneers had to make their own medicines and tend their own wounds and broken bones. And as more settlers made their homes on the south-west plains, bushrangers moved into the area. Holed up in the nearby Wedden Mountains, they stole horses, held up travellers on the roads, and raided homesteads for weapons and food. As protection, James White stocked the house with guns and bayonets and had portholes built into the side of the house for firing on intruders.

When Sarah was about 4, Thomas Whitton and another bushranger known as Scotchie raided Burrangong. Only Eliza White, her two little girls and the station manager's wife were at home: James White was away and the stockmen were out in the paddocks. Sarah was playing outside when several Aboriginal women raced by shouting 'Croppy come up!' before hiding in the bush. Sarah knew what that meant: bushrangers. As fast as her little legs could carry her, she raced back to the house. The thunder of hooves told her the bushrangers were close behind. The outlaws jumped off their horses and followed her into the house shouting orders. Then they forced the frightened women and children outside at gunpoint and lined them up. Scotchie guarded them with a gun while Whitton ransacked the house. The little girls howled with fright. To calm them down Scotchie went to his saddle-bag and took out a bag of boiled sweets. 'Bullseyes!' he said. The tears dried instantly: store-bought lollies were an unimaginable luxury out here. Their cheeks bulging with bullseyes, the girls watched the bushrangers rush out of the house laden with their uncle's guns and bayonets. Growling at the women to stay put, Scotchie and Whitton broke into the workers' huts and robbed them. Discovering a drum of rum, they called the stockmen in from the paddocks and made them drink the strong liquor at gunpoint. When the men were too drunk to be any threat, the bushrangers made their getaway.

Nobody at Burrangong had been hurt, but others in the region were not so lucky. When they left the Whites, Scotchie and Whitton galloped 32 kilometres to Currawong Station, where they shot five people, killing two of them. When James White returned home, he joined a search party to look for the outlaws, but they could not be found. After a reign of terror, Whitton was captured and hanged two years later after murdering John Hume, brother of the explorer, Hamilton Hume.

Until Sarah was 4, her parents lived and worked on Burrangong with her uncle. Then the family fell apart. In 1838 Eliza White went by carriage to visit Marengo, a nearby property. When she was due to return, John White walked out to meet her. But he became lost in the thick, trackless bush, and eventually died of thirst. After days of searching, James White found his brother's body, torn apart by wild dogs.

After her husband's death, Eliza White gave birth to a son called George. The following year she married George Groves, a farmer from Yass, and moved with him and her baby son to Victoria. Sarah and Eliza stayed at Burrangong with their Uncle James, who became their legal guardian. It's not clear why the girls didn't go with their mother. One theory is that Eliza White had been unfaithful to her husband before his death with George Groves, and that James White threw her out of the house and refused to let her take his nieces. Certainly, while her brother-in-law was alive, Eliza never returned to Burrangong, and it would be seventeen years before the girls saw her again.

Sarah White Musgrave

The loss of her father and her mother changed Sarah's life dramatically. She and Eliza were raised by James White and their aunt Sarah, who had sought refuge at Burrangong with two of her three children after Thomas White, James's older brother, was killed in an accident in Van Diemen's Land. James White never married, and raised his nieces as his own daughters. To Sarah, he was a hero. Most of all she admired his kindness — to herself and Eliza, to his workmen, and to the Aborigines. James was even kind to convicts on the road gangs, throwing them silver coins when he passed by on his way to Sydney to sell his wool.

Sarah did not have time to mope about her mother. With 800 cattle, 200 horses, 2500 sheep and forty stockmen, Burrangong was a busy, thriving enterprise. With no town nearby, the Whites had to grow their own wheat and barley and grind it to make bread. Everyone was expected to pull their weight, even the girls. They would get up at dawn to milk the cows, and helped their aunt churn the butter. Eliza preferred to work in the house, but Sarah was a tomboy. She learned to ride as soon as she could sit on a horse, and loved to chase around with the stockmen mustering sheep and cattle.

Despite James White's friendship with Cobborn Jackie, the south-west Aborigines remained a threat in the early days of white settlement. Though Sarah's uncle kept an arsenal of weapons, he never used them on the Aborigines: he preferred diplomacy. Each winter he handed out food and blankets, and when he went to Sydney, brought back knives, tobacco, tomahawks, clay pipes and red and yellow ochre for the Aborigines to use to paint their faces and bodies. But this backfired one year, when the Aborigines decided they wanted more. Out riding one day when her uncle was away, Sarah noticed a large band of Aborigines moving towards Burrangong. Knowing Eliza and her aunt were terrified of Aborigines, she spurred her horse, and set off for the homestead at a gallop. Reaching the house, she jumped down, tied up her horse, and ran inside.

'Close the window and bolt the doors, Eliza!' she shouted. 'There are hundreds of blacks on their way here!'

'What do they want?' asked her sister, her face ashen.

'I don't know. You two stay inside. I'll talk to them.'

Sarah was confident she could negotiate with the Aborigines. After all, she had been looked after by Aboriginal nurses, had played with the children, and spoke some of their language. But when she looked out the window and saw about a thousand Aborigines camped in front of the house, her heart sank. A small, wiry girl with pigtails in a faded dress and riding boots, Sarah went outside, murmuring a little prayer. A group of elders immediately stepped forward and demanded food.

'But you've already had your rations this year,' she said.

'We want more,' they said.

Realising that the confrontation could turn violent, Sarah agreed to cooperate. She and her aunt went into the store-room and brought out tea, sugar, tobacco, flour and meat for the elders. It wasn't enough, though; the Aborigines wanted more. Sarah took a deep breath. 'I can't give you any more,' she said. 'We need it ourselves.'

'Ask your uncle,' said a chief.

'Mr White is away,' said Sarah. 'And if you're still here when he gets back, he'll be very angry. I think you should go.'

'We stay,' said the Aborigines. 'This is our land.'

And sure enough, when James White returned and found the Aborigines camped in his front paddock, he was furious. But how could he make them leave without starting a shooting war? He had an idea. Loading his rifle, he went to the Aborigines' camp and shot two of their dogs. Terrified, the Aborigines grabbed the rest of their dogs and ran off into the bush, leaving a sick woman and her baby behind.

What would happen now? Would the Aborigines retaliate? The Whites soon found out. Some time later, 1500 screaming men in full war paint came rushing towards the house, brandishing spears, boomerangs and waddies. James White and his workers grabbed weapons, shoved the women inside, and backed up against the wall of the house, prepared for the worst. All Eliza's nightmares had come true; she moaned in terror. Sarah watched through one of the portholes. Then she spied their old ally at the head of the army. 'Eliza, look, there's Cobborn Jackie! He won't let them attack us.'

Because he trusted the chief, James White told his men to hold their fire. Then, miraculously, only 45 metres from the homestead, the Aborigines suddenly halted, squatted down, beat the ground with their waddies and burst into song. They were not going to attack! Sarah almost fainted with relief. Eliza burst into tears. Afterwards, Sarah discovered that Jackie, afraid the Aborigines would kill his old friend, had united the Murrumbidgee and Lachlan tribes and talked them out of retaliating. He then marched them 200 kilometres from the Snowy River to forgive James White for shooting the dogs. As a sign of goodwill, White had to attend an all-night corroboree. The abandoned woman and baby stayed at Burrangong and became part of the household.

But if the local Aborigines did not attack the Whites, they fought among themselves. In one battle, a warrior was decapitated by a boomerang, and

Sarah White Musgrave

two Murrumbidgee Aborigines were killed by the one spear, which passed through both of them. When Sarah was 7, Cobborn Jackie led the Lachlan-Murrumbidgee tribes into battle with the Namoi tribe on the plains. One of the family's Aboriginal workers was speared in this fight. His friends carried him 480 kilometres from Namoi back to Burrangong. James White gave him a hut and Cobborn Jackie nursed him faithfully, but his injury was too grave: six months later, when Sarah brought his lunch one day, she found him dead.

Unlike her sister, Sarah was fascinated by the Aborigines and their customs and rituals. She was horrified to see the women cut their heads with tomahawks and burn themselves with hot sticks to show their grief for the dead warrior. She also noticed that if a baby died, its mother had to carry the body around with her till a grown man had died. When a great chief died, Sarah went to the funeral. As he was buried, the women lowered into the grave bags containing the remains of four babies who'd died in the previous year. It was the chief's job to protect the babies on their way to the next life.

In 1843, when Sarah was 9, life at Burrangong became even harder. Gold had been discovered in California, and workers from all over New South Wales and Victoria walked off farms and stations and sailed to the American diggings to make their fortune. Their wives and children had to try to harvest the wheat and look after the stock. With the stockmen and bullock drivers gone, the Burrangong wool clip sat in the barn. James White had to soldier on as best he could. Fortunately, he had a first-rate worker in Sarah. She became the station's shepherd, guarding the sheep from dingoes and driving them back to the pens at night. Out in the paddocks by herself under the huge sky, she made up adventure stories with herself as the heroine, wondered what it would be like to have a mother, and day-dreamed about her future. Whatever the future held in store, she knew she wanted to stay right here on the plains where she belonged.

With her strong constitution and a good horse, Sarah weathered the first winter easily, but summer brought weeks of torrential rain. Burrangong Creek flooded and drowned some of the sheep, and the ground turned into a quagmire that bogged the horses and cattle. Unable to ride through the mud, Sarah had to follow the sheep on foot. It was a hard and unpleasant slog, but she was happy to do it for her uncle. Eventually, the Whites' stockmen returned, most of them poorer than when they left.

Then, when Sarah was 15, a terrible drought hit the area. For three years a relentless sun tortured the plains. After the first year the creeks dried up; eventually even the Lachlan River turned into a series of stagnant pools. Maddened by thirst, the cattle fought for every last puddle of water, and many were trampled to death. The creek beds were soon filled with dead beasts, and ravenous black crows feasted on the rotting carcasses. One by one the squatters gave up and walked off their land. Discouraged and bitter, many did not return even when the drought broke.

The Whites were lucky. Situated on the edge of the drought-stricken region, Burrangong escaped the worst. When the creek started to dry up, James White had wells dug, and discovered underground springs. By the time the drought ended, the stockmen had sunk wells from Burrangong to Chainy Ponds, a distance of 19 kilometres. During this ruinous drought Sarah again came to her uncle's aid. For a year she and a friend, Jane Robertson, helped keep the sheep alive by hauling up buckets of water from the wells and running it into troughs. It was back-breaking work. From dawn till ten at night they turned the heavy handle of the windlass, chatting and singing to keep their spirits up. Eliza did her bit by taking charge of the house.

When the rains came, the housekeeper at a nearby station asked Sarah, now 18, to visit to keep her company after the death of her son. At The Bland, Sarah met the station managers — John, William and Denis Regan. The Regan boys' parents,

Harriet and William Senior, had been transported to New South Wales as convicts in the 1820s. They settled on the Goulburn Plains, and prospered. They then bought The Levels near Burrangong, but before they could move onto the property, William Senior died. Five years later, leaving her three daughters in Goulburn, Harriet moved to the station with her three sons. She renamed it The Bland. After she died in 1844, her sons took over The Bland, but eventually sold up and stayed on as managers.

Soon after Sarah arrived at The Bland, the Lachlan River flooded. Within a few days the floodwaters had reached the homestead. Since John and William Regan were away, the task of saving everyone fell to Denis. He proved well up to the challenge, suggesting they all move to some nearby sand-hills, which stood higher than the floodwaters. But as the new overseer, Mr Carr, was too ill to brave the swirling torrent, they first had to move him, his wife and four children into the cramped and airless loft above the kitchen. To keep them comfortable, they rigged up a makeshift fireplace and brought in food supplies. Denis and a stockman then rushed off to the sand-hills and built mia-mias — shelters made out of branches — before wading back and helping Sarah and the housekeeper onto higher ground. The rain continued to pour down. It was too wet to light a fire, and the mia-mias leaked, but at least they were safe. After seven damp and dismal days the floodwaters finally began to recede. But the people in the house had suffered a dreadful ordeal in the dank, smoky attic; the overseer was gravely ill and his baby son unwell. The baby died a week later, and shortly after the overseer died of tuberculosis. Mrs Carr's father came and took her and the surviving children home with him.

Sarah's visit to The Bland during the flood had happy consequences; bonded by their adventure during the flood, she and Denis Regan fell in love. When Denis returned from mustering, he proposed and Sarah accepted. They were married in the Anglican church at Yass. The wedding party travelled the 113 kilometres to and from the ceremony on horseback. The newly-weds settled at The Bland, which Denis and William Regan were now managing while their brother John went exploring, opening up land farther west for settlement. As the only woman on the station, Sarah was faced with domestic chores for the first time in her life. Mrs Regan had trained her boys well, however, and Denis was able to teach her to cook.

It was a hard, lonely life for a young woman. But sometimes, when the men went out mustering and left Sarah alone, Eliza would ride over from Burrangong and keep her big sister company. This, too, had a happy outcome. Eighteen months after

Sarah's marriage, Eliza married Denis's brother, William. William was hired to manage Bland Creek Station nearby, and the two couples shared the Regan family homestead at The Bland.

Over the next five years, Sarah gave birth to two daughters, Harriet and Eliza. Now that they had children of their own, Sarah and her sister decided it was time to seek out their mother. By this time, George Groves had died, and their mother and half-brother were running Gobrup Station near Rushworth in Victoria. They set off on the long journey south through dry, dusty country for a reunion with their past. One cart contained Eliza, William and their month-old daughter; in the other were Sarah, Denis, their two girls and a nurse. They were away four months. It was a joyous reunion; although the girls had corresponded with their mother, they had not seen her or heard her voice since they were toddlers.

The Regans lived at The Bland for six years. But when James White's health began to fail, he asked Denis to manage Burrangong for him. Sarah was finally able to return to her old home. Before they took up their new position, the Regans went to Victoria to see Sarah's mother again. This was a much grander expedition. With her two young children, Harriet and Eliza, a nurse, a manservant and an Aboriginal helper, Sarah travelled in a large covered dray pulled by three horses, with ten spare horses trotting beside. Denis and Sarah's cousin, Thomas White, rode behind, driving 200 head of cattle. They suffered a setback at the Goulburn River Crossing in Victoria; the punt had sunk, meaning that the animals had to swim across. One bullock and seven of the spare horses were drowned, but they floated the dray with its three horses safely across the river on a pontoon of casks.

After a month's visit, the Regans returned to Burrangong. By this time James White had sold all his sheep, and had stocked his runs with cattle and horses. Life at Burrangong seemed perfect: the old man had Sarah and her family around him, and the property was doing well. But this peace was shattered in 1860, with the discovery of gold at Lambing Flat, one of James's cattle runs. Out rounding up wild horses, Denis and his stockman noticed that their horses were kicking up gold flecks on some rocks beside Burrangong Creek. They started panning in the creek, and immediately found gold nuggets. A few months later one of the stockmen reported the find to the government so he could claim a reward. When the *Sydney Morning Herald* broke the story, the Lambing Flat gold rush was on. Despite this, neither James White nor Denis Regan took out a licence to prospect for gold — they were cattlemen, not diggers.

Within a year, 30 000 diggers had poured into

James White's back paddock, turning it into a warren of trenches. The gold rush changed Sarah's life irrevocably. Burrangong's long isolation had ended — once in the outback, it was now next door to a noisy, dirty, tent city. Conditions at the diggings were primitive, and the water supply was soon polluted. Appalled at the suffering, Sarah brought several sick children to Burrangong and nursed them back to health.

The new settlement brought many social problems with it — theft, prostitution, illness, drunkenness, violence and racial strife. Most of the racial hostility was directed at the Chinese, who had flocked to Australia in the 1850s for the Victorian gold rushes and moved on to Lambing Flat. Many English and Irish settlers hated and feared the Chinese because they looked different, stuck together and were prepared to work for low wages. This resentment flared into violence in June 1861, when riots broke out. Led by a German band and waving the British, Irish, American and Lambing Flat flags, about 3000 men marched into the Chinese camp, wielding pick and axe handles, knives and guns. They looted and burned the Chinese settlement, then walked 10 kilometres to Back Creek and razed the Chinese camp there. Mounted miners pursued the fleeing Chinese, rounded them up and drove 1200 back on foot, beating them savagely and slashing off their pigtails. The government sent in fifty-seven police and thirty-six special constables to restore order, but when the police arrested the ringleaders, the miners attacked the police camp. In the battle that followed, one man was killed and twenty miners and several police were injured. The police released the five ringleaders, but the miners were still angry.

News of the riots flew around the stations on the plains. The squatters were afraid the violence would spread, but the crisis ended when the government sent mounted soldiers in to take charge. As it turned out, the only landowner directly affected by the riots was James Roberts, the owner of Currawong. When the miners drove the Chinese out, hundreds sought refuge on his property. He fed and housed them, and spent years trying to persuade the government to reimburse him.

The Lambing Flat gold strike dealt a great blow to James White's fortunes. Not only did he lose one of his most valuable cattle runs, he also ended up with a town almost on his doorstep — in 1861, Lambing Flat became the town of Young. When his workers deserted to the diggings, he had to bring out his sister, Janetta, and his nephew Frederick Taylor and his wife and five children from England to help him on the property. But if the gold rush was a shock, worse was to follow. In 1861 the New South Wales government passed a new law limiting squatters to 16 000 acres and allowing new settlers, or selectors, to take up small land holdings. James White had to stand by helpless as his vast land holdings were whittled down to 6500 hectares at Burrangong and the same at his second property, Curriberrima at Spring Creek.

Within a year, nearly five thousand selectors had taken up blocks of land ranging from 8 to 16 hectares. These small farmers began producing wheat, corn, barley and dairy products, and began to push further west, taking up bigger blocks. In the long run, grain brought far greater wealth to the area than gold.

Life was returning to an even keel when, in April 1863, Sarah suffered what she called 'the greatest calamity of my life': she lost her husband. Nine months after a fall from his horse while rounding up wild brumbies, Denis Regan died. Though Sarah nursed him tirelessly, she could not save him. A month later, her baby boy, George, died. At 29, with her uncle's health failing, Sarah found herself widowed with four children to raise — Sarah, Harriet, Eliza and Denis James. While she recovered, her English cousin Frederick Taylor kept the station going with the help of the stockmen. James White later hired William Regan, Sarah's brother-in-law, to manage Burrangong and Curriberrima.

Meanwhile, lawlessness increased on the goldfields. The lure of easy money attracted conmen, thieves and violent ex-convicts who came to prey on the hard-working miners. Horse theft was rampant, and bushrangers made the roads unsafe. The most daring and notorious of these was Frank Gardiner, a Goulburn boy. As well as holding up diggers, his gang made raids on homesteads in the district. Though he never threatened Sarah's family, Gardiner had a soft spot for Burrangong's excellent horses, and used the vast property as his headquarters.

Some months after Denis's death, while the men were away, Sarah had a visit from Gilbert and O'Meally, two bushrangers from Frank Gardiner's gang. Both were armed to the teeth. As she had known O'Meally since he was a boy, Sarah was wary, but not frightened. It turned out the gang wanted Sarah to prepare hot meals for them when they were in the area. She refused point blank, and tried to talk O'Meally out of rejoining Gardiner.

'It's too late, Mrs Regan,' said the bushranger. 'I've tried to go straight, but everybody knows my face now. The police will never leave me alone. I'm in to the finish.'

'I'll pray for you, John, and for your mother,' said Sarah, and watched them ride off.

But that wasn't the end of the saga. A passer-by saw Gilbert and O'Meally leaving the station and reported it to the police. A trooper was sent out to interview Sarah, and while he was there, three bushrangers rode up to the homestead, virtually straight into his arms. Instead of arresting them or trying to protect Sarah, however, the terrified trooper told her to lock the doors. Through a crack in the slabs of the house, Sarah watched the outlaws water their horses and ride off. Three years later, when Gilbert was shot, he was riding a valuable horse from Burrangong.

Though she missed Denis, Sarah had her children to worry about. Two years after his death, she married again. Her new husband was Thomas Musgrave, a selector from the other side of Burrangong Creek. While James White was alive, they lived at Burrangong, but when her uncle died in September 1865, Sarah and Thomas and the children moved to their new home, Musgrave House. Later they turned it into a hotel. James White's land was divided up between Sarah and Eliza's sons and their cousin, Thomas White. The old man's money was held in trust for his grand-nieces till they came of age. The legacy amounted to 5000 pounds each — a huge fortune.

Sarah bore three more children at Musgrave House — Thomas, Wallace and Rebecca. But in 1885, at only 49, Thomas Musgrave died. It was a turning point for Sarah. She left the Young district and moved to Sydney, where she set up house with her mother, Eliza. In her old age, Sarah was cared for by her daughter, Harriet Johnson, who bought her a house nearby in Auburn. In memory of her beloved old home, Sarah called it Burrangong.

Sarah White Musgrave

Sarah Musgrave in 1932 (aged 98). Photo courtesy Young Historical Society.

In her later years, Sarah Musgrave became something of a celebrity. She wrote her memoirs at the age of 92, and in 1928, at 94, she went back to Young to advise the producer of a film called *The Birth of White Australia*. Four years later she visited the town again for its Jubilee celebrations. Sarah of the south-west plains died in 1937, at the age of 103.

Australian Heroines

Rewriting the Past

Since Sarah Musgrave wrote her memoirs, her descendants have found out much more about the White family. They discovered that James, John and Thomas White were not free settlers, but convicts — horse thieves from a family of horse thieves in Berkshire, England. They had been transported in 1812, James for fourteen years for receiving stolen goods, and Thomas and John for life for horse theft. Their father, Charles, and brother, Joseph, were hanged in England for the same offence. Thomas was sent to Van Diemen's Land, now Tasmania, and James and John to Botany Bay. James White was first assigned to work for William Cox, who supervised the construction of the road over the Blue Mountains in 1814, and later to landowner George Singleton.

Instead of treating his sentence as a punishment, James White saw it as an opportunity. When he received his ticket of leave, he bought 250 hectares of land on the Hawkesbury. Driven out by the floods, he opened a slaughterhouse and butcher shop on the corner of King and George Streets in Sydney. When his convict past made it impossible for him to get another land grant close to Sydney, he pushed out beyond the frontier.

Sarah's father, John White, often used the alias John Exile. Assigned to William Hovell, he absconded while the explorer was away in New Zealand and signed on to the *Baring*, a ship bound for India. Captured and returned to Sydney in 1816, he was sentenced to hard labour and put to work on a convict gang building the new Parramatta Road — this is probably why James White used to throw coins to convicts working on the roads. Despite his constant breaches of discipline, John Exile received his ticket of leave in 1820, and was working in his brother's butcher shop when James White set off to pioneer the south-west plains.

May Zinga Wirth

The Greatest Horsewoman on Earth

May Zinga Martin before she took the name
Wirth — 'the world's greatest lady bareback rider'.
Photo courtesy Geoff Greaves.

May Zinga Wirth

Given away by her parents and adopted into Australia's biggest circus at 7, May Wirth became a peerless bareback rider. She went on to find fame and fortune in the United States with the Barnum and Bailey Circus — the Greatest Show on Earth — and the Ringling Brothers Circus.

May Wirth was born May Emmaline Zinga in Bundaberg, Queensland in 1894. Her father was a circus acrobat named John Despoges, who called himself Johnny Zinga. Johnny told people he was a Frenchman from Marseilles, but in fact he had come to Australia in his teens from Mauritius, a French-ruled island off the east coast of Africa. It was Johnny's dark skin that earned him his stage name. Circus folk had nicknamed him 'Zingaro', the Italian word for gypsy, and it had quickly been shortened to Zinga. May's mother, Dezeppo Marie Beaumont, had been raised by her father, a circus rouseabout, after her own mother's early death.

Johnny and Marie toured India and South-East Asia with a circus, but after May was born they settled in Australia. May was a typical circus kid. By the time she was 3 Johnny was teaching her tumbling and contortion tricks, and when she was 5 she made her first public appearance as a contortionist. By then she had two brothers and a sister.

In 1899 the Zingas joined the country's top circus, Eroni Brothers. With its 135 horses, 20 wagons, and scores of performers, musicians and tentmen, Eroni's travelled the backblocks of Queensland and New South Wales. Life in the circus was rough and ready. In the wet season, the horses had to pull the wagons through mud or flooded creeks; in the dry season there were droughts, dust storms and flies. Circus folk camped out under the stars, cooked over wood fires and had to boil water to wash, and many earned little more than their keep. But they quickly became addicted to the freedom of life on the road — the constant movement, the new places and faces — and the excitement of being in show business.

May's mother loved circus life, but found living with Johnny Zinga intolerable. Bad-tempered and brutal, he once chased her round the circus and dragged her back to their tent by the hair. In 1901, when May was 7, Marie ran away. As a single woman with children, she faced a bleak future. There was no market for acrobats in the 'real' world, and no such thing as unemployment benefits. To make a living she'd have to take in washing or clean people's houses. Marie made a hard choice: she decided to keep the three younger children and give May away.

In those days, children were often given to

May Zinga Wirth

relatives or friends to bring up if their families broke up or their parents died. Circus folk also took in unwanted and illegitimate children. Though they had to work hard and missed out on a decent education, these circus orphans had the security of belonging to a big 'family' and the freedom and fun of circus life. Most of them ended up as cheap labour, but the lucky ones were trained as acrobats, trapeze artists, trick riders or clowns.

Marie chose Marizles Martin to be May's new 'mother'. Born Mary Elizabeth Victoria Wirth, she called herself Marizles (pronounced Marilly), an old German family name, which everyone shortened to Rill. Rill was one of the Wirths, the famous circus family. Marie, who had worked for Wirth's Circus, admired Rill, who was convent-educated, well-spoken and elegant. It was a heart-breaking decision, but Marie believed her daughter would be better off with the Wirths, who were the aristocrats of the circus world — rich, respectable and Catholic. So in November 1901, Marie handed May over to Rill in Melbourne. Too young to understand her mother's reasons, May simply felt abandoned.

Rill took the confused little girl to Flinders Street Station, where they caught the train to Ballarat to join Wirth's Circus. It was clear that May had been neglected: she was grubby and had sores on her scalp. Horrified, Rill shaved off her thick dark hair and made her wear a cap. Distraught and humiliated, May howled. She cheered up, though, when Rill made her some new clothes.

May entered a new world when she became a member of the Wirth family. Although other circuses still travelled by horse-drawn wagon, the Wirths had their own train. May had never imagined such luxury. She lived with her new parents in their compartment and took lessons from the circus manager with her new cousins, Rill's nephews George, Alex and Eddie. She even had her own babysitter, Tommy Dean, a Cockney groom, who put up the ropes and pulleys for her training, and took her home at night and put her to bed.

May had to wait to meet her new sister, Stella. Two years older than May, Stella lived in Sydney with an aunt and attended Monte Sant' Angelo, a Catholic private school in North Sydney. Though Stella was being brought up a lady, it was made clear to May that she had to earn her keep. She would be groomed to be a circus performer; if she had talent, she might even become a star.

That Christmas vacation, May and Stella finally met. They took to each other immediately, and stayed close friends all their lives. The girls shared a passion for the circus. Stella, like May, had the circus in her blood — until the age of 7, she'd toured the world with Wirth's Circus. During the school

May Zinga Wirth

holidays she learned new tricks and performed alongside her parents. Though never in May's league, she did become a successful bareback rider and worked in circuses for most of her long life.

May didn't envy Stella her expensive private school and music lessons. The circus was her life. She loved everything about it — the easy camaraderie of circus folk, the travelling, and the thrill of performing in front of a crowd. She loved steaming into town on the circus train; the frenzied unloading, assisted by the circus elephant; the street parade; and the organised chaos of setting up the big top, digging the circus ring, erecting the rigging for the trapezes, and putting up the seats. And when May stood in the ring, the centre of all eyes, she felt like a princess, surrounded by the ringmaster in his tuxedo, the brass band thumping out circus tunes, the brave animal trainers with their lions and tigers, the clowns in full make-up and baggy pants, the tumblers in tights, the strong man, the equestrians on their gorgeous horses, and the trapeze artists in satin and spangles. She revelled in the tension and excitement of the crowd, the smell of the sawdust, the roar of the lions and tigers, the spit and hiss of the carbide lights, and most of all, the thrill of pulling off a perfect trick.

Determined to make a career in the circus, May set out to prove she was worth her keep. A gifted bareback rider herself and the only woman who could juggle on a galloping horse, Rill took over May's training. She kept May to a tough regimen, learning trapeze work, acrobatics, contortions, dancing and walking backward and forward on the tightwire with only a small Japanese parasol for balance. When May was small, Rill would help her practise balancing on her hands in the bedroom before breakfast. For fun May would join the other circus kids in the 'leaps', a competition to see who could somersault over the most horses, camels or elephants. The four Wirth children even developed their own side-show act, The Children's Circus.

When May was only 8, Rill decided she was ready to perform her contortion act in public. Little May, as she was billed, acted like a star from the very beginning. When the bandmaster forgot to give her a box of chocolates after her act one night, she refused to leave the stage until she received her tribute. The following year she made her first appearance on the tightwire.

In her spare time, May would watch Philip Wirth, her uncle, breaking in horses for the circus. When she turned 10, he asked her if she'd like to learn trick riding. The most difficult, demanding and dangerous act in the circus, bareback riding required strength, perfect balance and tumbling skills. Though May was only 150 centimetres tall, she was strong, with muscular legs and shoulders, and was blessed with

May Zinga Wirth

grace and excellent balance. But more importantly, May had the right temperament for bareback riding; daring, determined and fiercely ambitious, she would not rest until she had mastered a skill. May didn't want to be good, she wanted to be the best. She leapt at the chance.

Philip chose Silver Queen, a dappled cream pony with a broad back and a calm disposition, as May's training horse. He made her practise splits and taught her the basic bareback riding tricks: foot jumps; the flip flap — a backwards somersault onto two hands then back onto the feet; and the jerk — a reverse flip flap. All this was done bareback from the beginning, with no saddles or padding. It was hard and it could be scary, but May was resolute.

John Welby Cooke, an expert English bareback rider, took over May's training from her uncle. He taught her somersaults on horseback, including the breathtaking feet-to-feet forward somersault. As the rider lost sight of the horse during this somersault, it was highly dangerous and difficult to learn. May was the only woman who ever mastered this trick, and it would be enough to propel her into the big time.

After a year May could turn flip flaps on a galloping Silver Queen all the way around the circus ring. Eventually she could throw seven somersaults in a row, and as a finale, climb under and over the horse before clinging to its side. It was a demanding job.

Hours of practice on Silver Queen would leave May exhausted, dirty and sweaty. Even if she woke up stiff and sore from falls, she had to get up and start again. When she wasn't on a horse, May practised contortions to keep her body limber. By the time she was 12, she was performing five different acts in the circus under a variety of names — May Martin, Mayazel, Mademoiselle Mayonna, and even May Ringling. Eventually she took Rill's name and settled on May Martin Wirth, or just May Wirth.

It was in Wirth's Circus that May met her future husband, Frank White. Six years older and a dapper dresser, Frank started out selling tickets, played the bass drum in the band and ended up doing a clown act.

May's extraordinary talents should have made her an Australian show-business superstar. Everything was right but the timing: May was born too late. Equestrian acts had been immensely popular before the turn of the century, but audiences were tiring of them. They wanted something new and different, like animal acts. When May was in her teens, the most popular act in the country was a troupe of trained seals who could do the same tricks as humans and make the audiences howl with laughter as well.

Rather than see May's talents go to waste, her other uncle, George Wirth, decided to help her break into the American circus business. America had a

May Zinga Wirth

huge population and its circuses had an insatiable appetite for new acts. In 1910, when George was in the United States scouting for talent to bring to Australia, he told John Ringling — owner of America's biggest circus, Ringling Brothers–Barnum and Bailey — about May's skills. Impressed, Ringling wrote to Rill offering May an audition with Ringling Brothers Circus. When Rill read the letter to May and Stella, they whooped for joy. This was a once-in-a-lifetime opportunity. The girls begged Rill to let them go to America. There was nothing to hold Rill in Australia any more; her husband had died of tuberculosis four years earlier. She agreed.

On 9 June 1911, May, now 16, 18-year-old Stella and Rill boarded the *Makura* and sailed for America. It was a bittersweet parting for the girls — Stella was leaving behind her sweetheart, Phil St Leon, and May had to part from Frank White — but any sadness was quickly swept away by excitement. En route, the ship's crew discovered a stowaway on board — Tommy Dean, May's old babysitter. Rill paid his fare, and he joined the troupe. After taking a month's break in Honolulu to work in a theatre, the Wirths reached San Francisco and boarded a steam train for the two-day journey to New York. Will Rogers, a cowboy who'd appeared with Wirth's in Australia, met them at Grand Central Station. He later became famous as a homespun philosopher and humourist.

Rill booked them into a theatre folks' boarding house just off Broadway. Then they rushed out to explore New York, with its thronging crowds, its elevated railway, its famous Statue of Liberty, its huge department stores and, most importantly, its numerous musical halls and theatres.

Ouika Meeks, an American rider hired to replace May at Wirth's, had given them an introduction to Josie de Mott, one of the country's top trick riders. Josie generously invited them to her estate in Long Island — a refuge for New York's rich and famous east of the city — where she'd retired to train horses. They stayed there for several weeks, May using the time to train with Josie's horses on a circus ring in the grounds. It was at Josie's that May met one of the great loves of her life — a 6-year-old dappled grey horse called Joe. With his broad back, short legs and even gait, Joe was exactly what May needed in a horse. As a bonus, Joe liked women riders. The horse cost a fortune and Josie drove a hard bargain, but Rill gave in to May's pleas and bought the horse for her seventeenth birthday.

John Ringling finally made the journey to Long Island to see May ride. For the big audition, May had her hair bobbed, and Rill made her a new costume — blue satin with a tiny skirt and tight bodice decorated with sequined flowers. This was very daring at a time when most circus equestriennes wore much longer,

May Zinga Wirth

looser outfits, but these clothes were too dangerous for the advanced tricks May performed. Excited and a little nervous, she woke early. Unfortunately, it had rained overnight, and Josie's circus ring had turned into a giant mud puddle. Undaunted, May put on her new outfit and tied a big pink bow in her hair: it would become her signature.

Rill was worried about May riding on wet ground — the horse could easily slip and throw her. But May insisted on going on. How often did you get a personal audition with one of the most powerful circus moguls in the world? May won. Everything was going well until she attempted a forward somersault ... and missed. Embarrassed but unhurt, she landed in the mud at John Ringling's feet. He tried to talk her out of trying again, but May leapt back onto Joe and had another go. This time she executed the trick flawlessly.

John Ringling knew a star when he saw one. This package was perfect: a pretty young girl on a big horse doing stunts most men could not perform. Here was his top billing for the coming season. Over afternoon tea, he made May an offer she couldn't refuse — a season with Barnum and Bailey. Calling themselves 'The Wirth Family', the three Wirth women, Tommy Dean and Frank White — who'd travelled from Australia to be with May — signed up to perform at the 1912 season of 'the Greatest Show on Earth'. In the meantime, the Wirths toured Spain with a circus, landing in the middle of a revolution.

They arrived back in the United States in time for 'the call' for Barnum and Bailey performers to attend a week of rehearsals at Madison Square Gardens, the grand performing arts complex in New York City. As well as a huge production of Cleopatra, complete with elephants, tigers and richly costumed actors, the 1912 season featured May Wirth. She was billed as 'the world's greatest lady bareback rider, exhibiting feats of equestrianism never before attempted by a woman.'

May Wirth performing her backwards somersault. Photo courtesy Circus World Museum, Baraboo, Wisconsin, USA.

On opening night, as she waited in the wings, May was elated and anxious but perfectly in control.

She had put in many hard years of practice, and knew she could do this. The ringmaster announced her act; Frank wished her good luck; and May's honour guard of twenty-six Hussars on cream horses cantered into the ring. Then Tommy Dean led May, splendid in her blue satin and spangles, into the centre ring astride Joe. The lights over the two side rings went down, and thousands of pairs of eyes turned towards the petite girl on the horse. Rill took her position as ring mistress, dressed in silver. The band struck up May's music and she kicked Joe into a gallop. With an enthralled crowd holding its breath, she completed her routine faultlessly. Back in the wings, exultant and excited, May threw herself into Frank's arms: the whole world was at her feet now. Within a few weeks, everybody in New York knew May Wirth's name, and she and her Hussars were invited to lead a parade along Fifth Avenue.

When the Madison Square Gardens season ended, the Wirths packed up and joined the rest of the Barnum and Bailey entertainers on the road, performing under canvas across North America. They would headline the circus for two seasons in a row.

Always keen to learn new tricks, May took lessons from other expert riders in the circus. Orrin Davenport, one of America's best, taught her the 'back across', a somersault from the back of one horse to the back of another riding behind. The climax of this was a back flip into the centre of the ring. May was the first woman to perfect both this and the backwards somersault on a single horse. In this trick she would throw her body over, make a half twist, and land facing forward.

As famous as today's film and television stars, May's presence was soon felt way beyond the circus ring. At 18 she could go into a big department store and find hats, blouses and shoes named after herself. At a time when most women rode side-saddle in ankle-length skirts, America's best-known horsewoman rode astride in a skimpy costume. Asked why, she replied that side-saddles were unnatural, and caused internal injuries. Long skirts? They were a safety hazard, she said. In hitching her skirts, May was well ahead of her time — it wasn't until the 1920s that ordinary American women started wearing skirts above their knees.

Though May made her gravity-defying tricks look easy, the reality was very different. Turning somersaults on a galloping horse was dangerous. This came home to a Brooklyn audience in 1913, when May suffered the worst fall of her career from Kitty, the spirited mare she used for the finale of her act. Only recently broken in, Kitty was skittish, and when a property man distracted her, she bolted. Just coming out of her cowgirl sequence, May was lying across the horse's back with her head into the ring and her

May Zinga Wirth

weight supported by a rope through a stirrup. When Kitty took off, May was thrown against the wooden kerb of the ring and knocked unconscious, before falling between Kitty's hooves. Six thousand shocked people rose to their feet as May was dragged round the ring three times, her head banging against the kerb. A man tried to rescue her, but Kitty knocked him down in her panicked charge. The horse raced on till several property boys jumped into the ring and forced her to a halt. By this time May was unconscious, with a deep wound over her right ear. She was rushed to the wardrobe room and the circus doctor was called. The rumour raced round the audience, then the city, that May was dead. In fact, though she'd had a few teeth knocked out and suffered a broken nose, she was not seriously injured.

May's close call became a media sensation. John Ringling visited her every day, and flowers and sympathy cards poured into her hotel room. But May was determined not to let the accident interrupt her career for too long. After a month's lay-off, she started practising again. It was probably too soon, for she quickly had another accident. This time Kitty slipped on a water-soaked ring in St Louis and threw May so hard she landed outside the ring, twisting her knee. Against Rill's advice, she went back on and finished her act. As a result, the knee never healed properly, and gave her trouble all her life.

The Wirths left Barnum and Bailey in July 1913, and May convalesced at Josie de Mott's estate. When she had recovered, they went to London to appear at the Wonder Zoo and Circus at the Olympia theatre. Twice as big as Madison Square Gardens, the Wonder Zoo seated 5000 people and featured many of the world's top circus acts. To get to their seats, the audience had to pass thousands of animals, not in cages, but in 'natural' settings — lions in trees, polar bears on rocks. The Wonder Zoo boasted the cream of the equestrian world. Besides May, there were rough-and-tumble riders, a Circassian rider, a couple with a squadron of 150 trained horses, and the star of the show, a Danish girl called Baptista Schreiber on a white stallion from the Danish Royal Stable.

After London, the troupe visited France, but cut the tour short when war broke out in Europe in 1914. Although they had intended to go back to the United States, it became impossible to get the horses onto a ship. Rather than be stranded in London, Rill decided they should go home and do a season with Wirth's Circus in Australia. Frank and Tommy had to sail via South Africa with the horses, while May, Stella and Rill travelled via New York and Vancouver. They arrived in Sydney on 21 September 1915.

The trip was a disappointment for May. A huge star in America and Europe, she was just another trick rider to Australia's blasé audiences. Horses were

May Zinga Wirth

ho-hum in a country where so many people still rode well. After her first performance in Wirth's new Hippodrome in Melbourne, May broke down and cried. But rescue was at hand. The Ringling Brothers wanted the Wirth Family back and were prepared to pay handsomely for the privilege. When the war started, many of Ringling's European performers had returned home, leaving the American circus desperate for high-quality acts. Before they returned, Rill signed up Phil St Leon, Stella's boyfriend, as their male trick rider. The troupe reached the United States on Boxing Day, 1916.

After a season at Ringling's, the Wirths toured Cuba. By this time, Frank had left the group to open an agency in New York to book acts for Wirth's Circus in Australia. After the war ended in 1918, he travelled Europe scouting for talent. In November the following year, May married her childhood sweetheart in The Little Church Around the Corner in New York. John Ringling gave May away. Though May loved Frank, she did not let marriage get in the way of her first love — bareback riding. While May went off touring with the Wirth Family, her new husband, calling himself Frank Wirth, stayed in New York to pursue his career.

By now, May and her troupe were earning big money. They'd come a long way from the Spartan conditions of their first season with Barnum and

Bailey, when they had to share a dressing tent with dozens of other performers and were given only two buckets of cold water a day for bathing and laundry. Ringling Brothers was like a small town — with 1500 inhabitants, including performers, tradesmen and labourers — criss-crossing the country by train. As stars, the Wirths now travelled in style, with their own apartment in a Pullman carriage on the Ringling train. Their quarters boasted a living room, two bedrooms and a kitchen and bathroom, all decorated to suit their own tastes. Stella took her piano with her, and the circus management transported May's dashing touring car on the train.

In 1921 the Wirth Family left Ringling's, but returned for the 1924 to 1927 seasons. Meanwhile, Frank's career had flourished, and he and May bought an estate on Long Island. May had intended to retire from performing in 1934, when she turned 40, but had second thoughts when Frank got into financial difficulties. When the family decided to form a new circus, she joined up. She could still wow a crowd, but could no longer do the difficult backwards and forwards somersaults. Three years later she retired permanently, and went to work with Frank in his booking agency. Though she returned to Australia several times, she never moved back. Australia had changed and moved on without her, and all her friends were in America. The rest of the Wirth

May Zinga Wirth

Family stayed in America, too. Rill lived in New York till her death in 1948; Stella and Phil worked for Hunt Brothers Circus till Phil's death in 1958.

Few Australians seemed to remember or care who May Wirth was. In fact, circuses were dying out here. In 1963 even Wirth's once-great circus stumbled to a halt, the victim of television and changing tastes in entertainment. But the American circus industry recognised May's importance, and in 1964 admitted her to the Circus Hall of Fame in Sarasota, Florida. (Only two other Australians made it into such august company: Con Colleano, the famous tightwire walker, and his sister Winnie, a trapeze artist.)

In 1965 both Frank and Stella died, Frank from lung cancer, and Stella after a fall on her return from a last trip home to Australia with May. Alone now, May moved to Sarasota, the headquarters of Ringling Brothers, and the favourite retirement town of old circus folk. After an extraordinary life, full of challenge and adventure, she died in 1978. May

May Wirth on a stamp to commemorate the 150th anniversary of the circus in Australia. Courtesy National Philatelic Collection, Australia Post.

127

Wirth was one the last great equestrians, and probably the greatest woman trick rider of all time. It wasn't until 1997 that May's home country honoured her genius — on a stamp commemorating 150 years of the circus in Australia.

This story was drawn from Mark St Leon's unpublished book, *The Bareback Queen: The Story of May Wirth*.

Molly Craig

Escape from the Moore River
Native Settlement

Molly Kelly at Jigalong in 2000. Courtesy Doris Pilkington.

Taken from their families in the north-west of Western Australia in 1931, three part-Aboriginal girls — Molly Craig, 14, Gracie Fields, 11, and Daisy, 9 — escaped from the infamous Moore River Settlement north of Perth. They walked home through 1600 kilometres of rough terrain, living off the land and dodging search parties all the way. Their extraordinary nine-week journey is one of the longest walks in the history of the Australian outback.

Molly Craig was born in the Pilbara region in Western Australia to an Aboriginal mother and a white father. Her Aboriginal family had come in out of the desert and settled at Jigalong, a base for maintenance men who worked on the famous rabbit-proof fence. Molly's mother, Maude, was the first girl from the Mardudjara tribe trained as a domestic worker by the Superintendent at Jigalong, and her father, Thomas Craig, was an English maintenance inspector on the rabbit-proof fence. Built in 1907 by the Western Australian government in a doomed attempt to stop rabbits from the east swamping the state's grazing lands, the famous rabbit-proof fence stretched 1834 kilometres from the Southern Ocean near Esperance

Molly Craig

to Eighty Mile Beach north of Port Hedland. Pairs of maintenance men riding horses or camels and working out of small depots had to keep 240 kilometres of fence free of damage by flood, fire, emus and kangaroos. The rabbit-proof fence became a landmark for blacks and whites alike.

Because of her light skin colour, Molly was shunned and insulted by the other children at the Aboriginal camp outside Jigalong. To make up for this, Molly's mother spoiled her; her grandfather, Willabi, took her on hunting trips with him; and her step-father, Galli, taught her how to handle herself in the bush. When Molly was 4, her life changed for the better; her two aunties gave birth to baby girls fathered by white men. Her new companions were Daisy, born at Mad Donkey Well, south-west of Jigalong, and Gracie — the daughter of Lilly and Alf Fields — who was born at Walgun Station to the north. When Gracie's family moved to Jigalong, she and Molly became inseparable. Then, after her parents began working on Murra Murra Station, Daisy became a regular visitor.

Unfortunately for the girls, Mr Keeling, the Superintendent of the depot at Jigalong, had noticed the way the other Mardu children treated them. Keeling was also a Protector of Aborigines — that is, it was his job to dispense food, clothing and blankets to the Aborigines in his care, and keep an eye out for their welfare. Concerned for the girls, he recommended to the Department of Native Affairs in Perth that they be removed from Jigalong. He later changed his mind, but by that time it was too late: the wheels of bureaucracy in Perth had been set in motion and nothing — neither his arguments nor the pleas of the grief-stricken families — could stop them.

Because the Aboriginal population had decreased so dramatically after white settlement, most people assumed that the Aborigines would die out. In most states, however, the number of part-Aborigines was increasing. By the late 1920s, the Western Australian government decided that the existence of what they called 'half-castes' was a problem. Because partly white children were regarded by white people as superior to traditional Aboriginal people, it was considered wrong for them to be brought up as Aborigines. The government decided to remove them from their parents and raise them as whites. They were encouraged to intermarry so that their black blood would be diluted, and their descendants would become white. Brutal and inhuman methods were employed to execute this policy. Patrol officers in cars and on horseback combed the outback hunting down part-Aboriginal children. They were taken away to institutions — Carralup Settlement near Katanning in the south-east or the Moore River Native Settlement, 130 kilometres north of Perth — where

Molly Craig

they were taught how to read, write and count, and trained as farm labourers or domestic servants. Many never saw their families again.

When the police were on the hunt, Aboriginal parents hid their children in the bush or rubbed them down with charcoal to make them darker. Sometimes it worked, but few children escaped for long. Eventually, the police caught up with Molly, Gracie and Daisy. In July 1931 Constable Riggs, the feared Protector of Aborigines, rode into the Mardu camp outside Jigalong to collect the girls. Only Molly and Gracie were there; Daisy was on another property. The policeman told the girls' grandfather he was taking them to the Moore River Native Settlement near Perth. That meant nothing to people who had never been out of the Pilbara. Bewildered and terrified, Molly and Gracie were heaved onto the policeman's spare horse for the trip back to Jigalong. As the little group rode off, the Aborigines in the camp began to wail and cry. To show their grief, they gashed their heads and bodies with sharp stones. Blood mixed with the tears on their faces and dripped into the red dust. Molly and Gracie watched helplessly.

At Jigalong, Riggs picked up two sick Aboriginal women, Nellie and Mimi-Ali, who had a badly broken leg, and loaded them and the girls into his car for the trip to Marble Bar. It was the first time Molly and Gracie had ever ridden in a car. Before leaving the district, the trooper stopped off at Walgun Homestead, where he found Daisy at a bush camp. Because it was too late to push on, the cousins were able to spend one last night at the camp with Gracie's mother Lilly and granny Frinda before they were wrenched away. Amid wailing and lamentation, they set off early next morning. Gracie's white father stood by watching, but made no move to save his daughter. Disgusted, Gracie's mother soon left him and moved to Wiluna.

Eventually, exhaustion overtook the girls and they slept. When they woke, they were on the main road to Nullagine. They whispered among themselves, trying to make sense of it all, but all they knew was that they were being taken away to school. At two o'clock on 21 July they reached Marble Bar, where Nellie was admitted to hospital. Mimi-Ali and the girls were handed over to Constable Melrose, who looked after them in the Marble Bar police station for several days while they waited for the train to Port Hedland.

The steam train, the Spinifex Express, frightened them when it clanged into the station and blew its whistle, but with its velvet seats, water bottles and framed photos of places they'd never been, it was much more comfortable than the car. And the journey gave them their first, thrilling sight of the

Molly Craig

sea. After huffing its way down the coast for eight hours, the train reached Port Hedland, where another policeman took Mimi-Ali and the girls to a wharf and handed them over to the captain of the *Koolinda*, a government ship. They were on their way to Fremantle, the constable said. Transfixed by the sight of the ship, the girls scarcely heard him. What were they in for now, they wondered.

They soon found out. When the *Koolinda* reached the open sea and began to pitch and roll, the girls became seasick and were sure they were going to die. But they gradually got used the motion and fell into an exhausted sleep. When they awoke, all they could see through the porthole was endless blue water. A stewardess collected them, fed them breakfast and took them out on deck to watch big fish jumping out of the sea. The crew were kind, but the girls were too dazed and shy to respond. After five days at sea, the *Koolinda* reached Fremantle, which was cold and wet. The stewardess gave each of the shivering little girls a comb, a mirror and a mysterious clammy garment which turned out to be a raincoat.

The bustle, the ships, the cranes, the trucks and the noise of the busy port were alarming, but Mimi-Ali's ambulance quickly whisked them away to Perth. Noses pressed against the ambulance windows, they gaped at the tall buildings, the sleek cars, the clanking trams, and crowds of people. Before they knew it they had arrived at the East Perth Girls' Home, where they stayed overnight before the final leg of their long journey. The newcomers were quickly surrounded by other Aboriginal girls. The girls said they were in Perth to get an education, too, and when they finished, they'd be going home — in fact, most of them ended up working on farms far from their homes and families. Early the next morning the cousins set out by car for the Moore River Native Settlement, 130 kilometres away. They arrived in pelting rain to find the road to the settlement under water. Alighting from the car, the girls stared around. Daisy's hand stole into Molly's. What sort of place was this?

Though the Moore River Native Settlement was established in 1917 as an internment camp for *nyoongars* — the south-western Aborigines who had been living in reserves or camps on the fringes of white towns — the first inmates were from the Pilbara. By the time Molly, Gracie and Daisy got to Moore River, it was starved for funds and had become overcrowded, rundown, unhealthy and dangerous. As well as a school for boys and girls, it was a dumping ground for part-Aborigines from all over Western Australia, home to orphans, old men and women, prisoners discharged from Fremantle Prison, unmarried mothers and incurably ill people. As the wages were low and the conditions poor, it had

Molly Craig

trouble attracting suitable staff. To help maintain discipline, several Aboriginal men — who came from other regions and had no obligations to the Aborigines at Moore River — were appointed as trackers or unofficial police. These brutal men reported on the residents, tracked down escapees on horseback and meted out punishment to those locked up in the prison hut. They patrolled the grounds armed with truncheons and big sticks, and would flog girls for offences as trivial as staying late in the dormitory.

A self-contained village by a river, the Moore River Settlement was set in 4 hectares of cleared land surrounded by pristine forest. In the centre of the compound stood the Big House, the Superintendent's home. In front of it ran the main street, flanked by the nursing sisters' quarters; the girls' and boys' dormitories; the sewing room, where girls over 13 had to work long hours making clothes for the residents and for sale outside; the dining room, bakehouse and kitchen; a kindergarten and the school, where an untrained teacher laboured to educate up to a hundred children of all ages. At the end of the compound, up the hill, was the Anglican Church, and next door to it was the Deputy Superintendent's house. Just before the church, a road branched off to Mogumber, 13 kilometres away. The settlement also had its own hospital, mortuary and cemetery. And down by the

A group of Aboriginal children outside the church hall at the Moore River Native Settlement. Courtesy Battye Library.

river was a camping ground for about two hundred adults, many of them the parents of children in the compound. They lived in tents and humpies made of iron and wood with dirt floors, and worked around the settlement.

While the children went to school, the young adults were trained to work: sewing, washing, ironing, doing maintenance work and labouring on the farm. Adults who could support themselves were encouraged to go out to work, while the old and sick had to survive somehow in the camp on the grounds. No one was allowed to leave without the government's permission.

Molly, Gracie and Daisy had no time to take in

Molly Craig

their new surroundings. A matron led them to a wooden building, where they waited while she undid the padlock and chain on the door. Was it a jail? No, it was a dormitory, housing about thirty beds in two rows separated by a passage. More than twenty sets of eyes turned to look at the newcomers. The cousins stared back, hardly hearing the matron telling them to choose a bed. If they needed to go to the lavatory, there was a bucket in the bathroom, she said. Then the matron left. After standing around uncertainly for a few minutes, the girls found beds, crawled in and tried to sleep. It was freezing: the beds had no sheets or pillowcases and only one blanket. Gracie soon sneaked into Molly's bed to get warm, and Daisy followed. They spent the night huddled together like sardines under their blankets, at the mercy of exhaustion, despair and the bedbugs, which made their home in the mattress.

At six the next morning, the girls were woken by a blast of cold air: the matron had pulled the blankets off them. They were immediately surrounded by curious girls wanting to know where they came from, who their families were. They washed and the old hands showed them how to make their beds. Martha Jones, a teenager from Port Hedland, took the trio under her wing and explained the rules. At seven the bell rang, and the girls fell in behind the others and marched single file through the drizzle to the dining hall for their first meal in their new home. Meanwhile, the boys were streaming out of their hut across the compound. Breakfast turned out to be weevilly porridge and bread and dripping, washed down by a mug of lukewarm, sweet, milky tea. Unable to taste a mouthful, the girls ate it sitting on long benches at refectory tables.

That afternoon, when the rain cleared, Martha and another girl, Polly Martin, took the cousins for a walk in the muddy grounds. They passed a group of children playing rounders and followed a trail along the cliffs overlooking the Moore River. Though the river was icy, brown and fast-flowing from the storm, some teenage girls and children were wading across. The eldest girl was showing the others how to use a stick to measure the depth of the water. It gave Molly an idea.

On their way back a girl's voice called out from a little stone hut begging for food.

'What's that?' asked Molly.

'The boob,' said Martha.

'What's a boob?'

'Kids who do really bad things get locked up there and fed on bread and water,' explained the older girl.

'What sort of bad things?' asked Molly, eyes wide.

'Like trying to escape,' said Martha.

She told them about a group who made it as far as the railway line between Gillingarra and Mogumber

Molly Craig

before they were caught by an Aboriginal policeman on horseback. 'He whipped them,' she whispered. When the kids were brought back, their heads were shaved and they had to parade around the compound in disgrace, she added. Back in the dormitory trying to warm up, Molly, Gracie and Daisy discussed what they'd seen and heard. They were struck dumb when one of their room-mates told them to speak English, that they'd be punished if they spoke 'blackfulla language'.

Lunch and dinner were watery stew with bread and treacle. This stodgy, unhealthy diet never varied. The settlement did not grow its own vegetables, and there was a shortage of meat, fruit and eggs. Molly saved her crusts and told the others to keep theirs, 'for later'. Mystified, Gracie and Daisy exchanged a look. What was Molly up to now? It was simple: Molly had decided to escape from this freezing prison with its bad food and its rules and regulations. Fourteen now, Molly was a *durn-durn*, a girl who had reached puberty and had been allocated a husband. At home she'd be working on a station, not going to school. She had no intention of staying here. Back in the dormitory, after roll call and lights out, she started planning. Though the thought of the boob made her shudder, she decided it was worth the risk.

Early next morning, she told Gracie and Daisy that they were going home to Jigalong.

'But how?' asked the little girls, astonished.

'We'll walk,' said Molly.

'But we don't know the way!' said Gracie.

'And it's so far ...' added Daisy, whose legs were short.

'We'll just find the rabbit-proof fence,' said Molly. 'Then we'll follow it all the way home.' She was confident she could do it. Her English father and her grandfather Willabi both worked on the rabbit-proof fence, and her Aboriginal step-father was an expert bushman.

Frightened at the enormity of disobeying the authorities and the prospect of such a long trip on foot, the two younger girls looked at each other for guidance. Martha had told them no girls had ever got away from Moore River and stayed free, and the story of the policeman and his stockwhip had struck fear into their hearts. But how would they survive in this terrible place if Molly left them? They agreed to go.

After an unappetising breakfast on that cold day at the beginning of August 1931, three tense girls packed their meagre possessions — Lifebuoy soap, a mirror, a comb — into their calico bags and tied them around their necks. Then they put on two dresses, two pairs of calico bloomers and a coat. But after further thought, Molly made them take off their coats despite the cold; heavy clothes would only slow them down.

Molly Craig

Then they ran. Molly urged the little girls on. They mustn't get caught now. Remembering what she'd seen yesterday, she scouted the river bank, using a stick to test the depth of the water. Finally she found a natural crossing place — a tree forming a bridge. They crossed, sloshed along the muddy banks for another two hours, then rested. They were a long way from the rabbit-proof fence, but Molly was sure she could find it. On the way into Moore River, she'd memorised the directions: north by car from Perth to Mogumber Siding, then west to the settlement. She'd also taken note of the position of the sun on her walk around the grounds the day before. She was positive they were heading in the right direction.

That first day they walked over wet grasslands and sand plains covered with acacias and prickly grevilleas that whipped at their bare legs, climbing boundary fences along the way. They emerged onto heathlands full of wildflowers, then open forests of banksias, prickly bark and Christmas trees. Once, frightened by running footsteps, they hid in the bushes and watched a black figure run by. 'It's a *marbu*,' whispered Gracie, teeth chattering, thinking it was an evil spirit. It was probably an Aboriginal man running to get out of the rain, but they'd had a bad scare.

That night they camped in some sand dunes, digging into a deserted rabbit burrow to make a warm, dry shelter. Dinner was stale crusts and fresh water. After falling into an exhausted sleep, they were woken next morning by the thrum of rabbits in a nearby burrow. Hungry, Gracie caught one of the rabbits and killed it, but they had no matches to cook it.

Tired and hungry, and still upset by the close call with the *marbu*, Gracie wanted to go back — it was all too much for an 11-year-old who'd never been away from her family before. Eventually Molly managed to coax her into continuing. They plodded on through the rain till they reached a river, a tributary of the Moore River. The little girls squatted down and stared at the rushing water, ready to give up. But Molly would not be deterred. She found a fence that crossed the river and began inching her way across clinging to the wire. The others followed, and they all made it safely to the other side, their dresses tucked into their bloomers and their calico bags around their necks.

On the second day, in an area that had been burnt by bushfire, the runaways spied two Mardu men coming towards them, carrying a cooked kangaroo and two goannas. The girls' mouths watered. The men greeted them and gave them a kangaroo tail and one of the goannas. They also warned the girls that an infamous Mardu policeman, an expert black-tracker from the Kimberley, was probably already on their trail. If he found them, they'd get a flogging. As

Molly Craig

the tribesmen were leaving, the younger man gave them a precious gift — a box of matches.

They trudged on till dusk, when Molly let them make camp. Unlike the Pilbara, this countryside had plenty of trees, so the girls gathered wood and lit a fire. After roasting and eating the kangaroo and goanna, they settled down beside the fire to sleep. But the hardships were beginning to take their toll. They'd been covering about 24 to 30 kilometres a day, and were tiring. The next day Gracie informed them she was not going to walk any more. But when Molly and Daisy decided to soldier on, she had no choice but to follow, silent and unhappy. She perked up only when Molly spotted a rabbit warren — food! The girls stopped up all but one of the burrows and waited, and when the rabbits emerged, they chased them down. Molly and Gracie caught one each. That night they feasted on rabbit. Maybe life wasn't so bad after all.

The next day Molly heard a strange sound and urged the girls under cover. As they hid in the bush, the noise got louder and seemed to be coming from the sky. It was a plane, the first one the girls had ever seen. 'Are they looking for us?' asked Gracie. Molly nodded. From now on they'd have to be doubly careful. Later that day, plodding on, wondering if they'd ever reach home, the girls heard familiar noises and realised they'd come upon a farmhouse.

Molly sent her cousins ahead to ask for food, while she waited under cover. Spotting them from the verandah, a little girl asked them to come inside. Shyly, they refused. The girl summoned her mother. A kindly woman, Mrs Flanagan had already heard about the runaways, and felt sorry for them. She fed them and gave them tea leaves, half a leg of mutton, flour, salt, a chunk of fruit cake, bread and three large empty tins to use as billycans. In a store-room she found an old military greatcoat for Molly and wool jackets for Gracie and Daisy, and showed them how to make capes from flour bags to keep off the wind. Most importantly, Mrs Flanagan gave them some advice. 'You're going the wrong way,' she said. 'If you're looking for the rabbit-proof fence, you have to go east first,' — she pointed — 'then north.' The girls thanked her and set off. After they left, the woman started to worry. If something happened to them out there in the wilderness, it would be her fault. She called the police.

On 11 August 1931 a story about the girls' escape appeared in the *West Australian* newspaper. They'd been spotted passing New Norcia, but after a week of searching, all the police found was some discarded rabbit. Now the whole state was on the alert for the runaways. As the girls moved north, farmers reported seeing them, though nobody could catch them.

Molly Craig

Once, when they came upon a station out-camp — a tin shack with two camp beds and some supplies — the two little girls went in as usual. They found matches, flour, salt and three large Sunshine milk tins. When they prised the lids off they discovered the tins were full of dripping. Starving, they gorged on the fat. But when they reached Molly's hideout, they vomited it all up — it was too rich. They consoled themselves with damper and sweet black tea.

Often cold, hungry and exhausted, with the scratches on their legs from the prickly bushes infected and throbbing, the girls trekked on. They'd been running for a month. When Daisy could no longer walk, Molly piggybacked her, and the two younger girls took turns piggybacking each other just to get a rest. By sleeping from sunset to first light — 'piccaninny dawn' — they managed to stay ahead of the police search parties, but were afraid to light fires and attract attention.

Then, at long last, they reached the rabbit-proof fence. Molly was wildly excited. 'We're nearly home!' she shouted. In fact, they had only reached the halfway mark, and had another 800 kilometres to go. Sobering up, they set off again. Shortly after, a voice hailed them, and they looked around to see a strange sight: an Aboriginal stockman on a bicycle. It was Don Willocks, who worked at Pindathuna Station.

Frightened, they ran into the bush, but the man coaxed them out by offering them some of his sandwiches and a box of matches. But when the stockman left them, he reported the incident to his boss, who phoned the Yalgoo police. The police rushed to the site with an Aboriginal tracker, but were too late. It was the first week in September, and the girls were entering the territory of the Sandstone Aborigines.

Realising they were getting close to home, Molly adopted evasive tactics. They'd approach a farm or station from one direction and pretend to go off in another before doubling back and continuing on their relentless push north. They also stayed well away from towns. Reaching Mount Russell Station, several days past Meekatharra, Gracie learned from an Aboriginal woman that her mother had left Walgun Station and was living in Wiluna. That was enough for Gracie. She set off to find Lilly.

Molly and Daisy went on alone. Close to home now, with the weather warming up, they discarded their army coats. One day, while Molly was resting and Daisy bird-nesting, a part-Aboriginal stockman saw them and threatened to turn them in to the police. He retreated when Daisy swore at him and pelted him with stones, but he had given them a bad fright. They hurried on, stopping at midnight to light a fire and cook the birds Daisy had caught.

Molly Craig

They were now on their own land. They could almost smell home. And when they climbed the boundary fence of Station 594, a cattle station on the Canning Stock Route, they knew Jigalong was not far away. Hope gave them a second wind. Eventually, worn out and famished, they reached the camp of their aunt, Molly's stepfather's sister. There they had their first warm bath since leaving the East Perth Girls' Home nine weeks before, and filled up on beef stew and home-made bread. Around the camp-fire that night their relatives listened wide-eyed to their stories of life on the run.

They covered the last stretch in high style, on a camel. It belonged to their cousin Joey's boss, a contractor on the rabbit-proof fence. Taking turns riding on the fencers' camel, Molly and Daisy soon entered a familiar landscape — red earth, dry spinifex grass and grey mulga with purple hills in the distance. Two days later, they were home! They'd been away for almost three months.

After a corroboree to celebrate their return, the girls' families went bush. By now they were famous and everybody — including every policeman and black tracker in the state — was on the lookout for them. But the publicity had one unexpected result: A O Neville, the Chief Protector of Aborigines, decided he wanted nothing more to do with a troublesome and expensive girl like Molly, and left

Australian Heroines

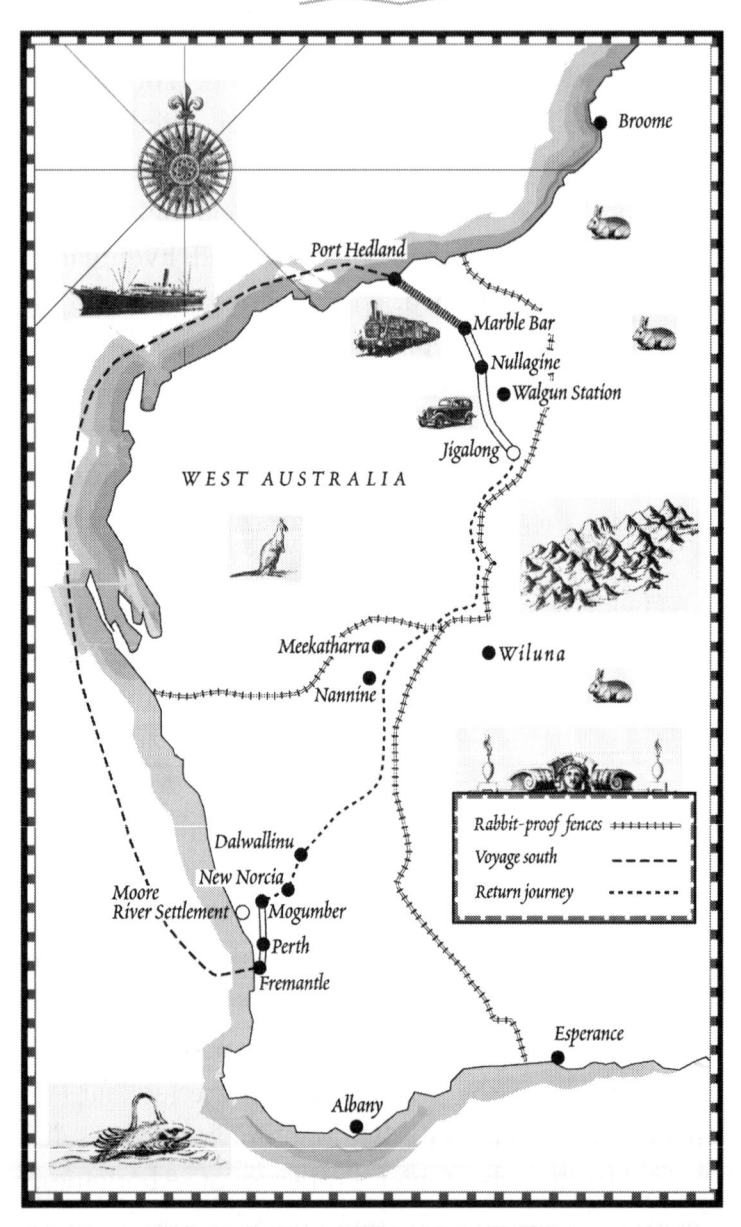

Map showing Molly Craig, Gracie Fields and Daisy Kadibil's journey from Jigalong in the Pilbara Region to the Moore River Native Settlement north of Perth and their epic 1600-kilometre trek home. Map drawn by Stanish Graphics.

Molly Craig

her alone. She became a domestic helper on Balfour Downs Station, married a stockman called Toby Kelly, and had two daughters — Doris and Annabelle.

Molly's freedom did not last, however. After being discharged from hospital in Perth after an appendicitis operation, she was whisked off to the Moore River Native Settlement. It was like a recurring nightmare. But Molly had lost none of her spunk. On 1 January 1941 she absconded, carrying her 18-month-old daughter Annabelle with her but leaving 4-year-old Doris at the settlement. Taking the same route the three girls had followed nine years before, she carried her baby 1000 kilometres to Meekatharra. There she picked up a lift which took them the rest of the way home. After months away, she arrived back at Jigalong and moved in with her husband at Balfour Downs. Three years later little Annabelle was removed and sent to Sister Kate's Children's Home in Queen's Park. Her mother has not seen her since. Since her retirement, Molly has lived at Jigalong.

Gracie Fields was captured at Wiluna and sent back to Moore River, where she was given the surname Jigalong. After finishing her education, she worked on farms and stations as a domestic help. She married Harry Cross and had six children, but never returned to Jigalong. She died in 1983.

Daisy moved with her family to the Jimbalar goldfields, then to a camp near Lake Naberu, south of Jigalong. She worked as a housemaid on various stations, and married Kadibil, a station hand, and had four children. After her husband's death, she moved to Kalundi Seventh Day Adventist Mission north of Meekatharra and remained there till it closed in the 1970s. Daisy Kadibil now lives with her son and daughters and their families at Jigalong.

Molly Kelly's daughter, Doris, was subsequently moved from Moore River to Roelands Mission. At 18 she left to train as a nursing aide at the Royal Perth Hospital, married, and lived in Geraldton with her husband and six children. When Doris was 26, she was reunited with her mother and father at Meekatharra. She later studied journalism at Curtin University, and in 1996 wrote the story of her mother's adventure in *Follow the Rabbit-Proof Fence*. It has now been made into a film.

Molly Craig

The Desert Aborigines

White settlers pioneered Australia's west in 1829. It took another fifty years for cattle and sheep farmers to reach the north-west and begin pushing inland. The Pilbara — a region of some 510 000 square kilometres reaching from Exmouth in the south to Eighty Mile Beach in the north — was opened up by gold miners in the 1860s. Till then, the Aboriginal tribes who ranged across the Pilbara had remained untouched by white culture.

Pilbarra is an Aboriginal word for stream, but though rivers dominate the western part of the region, the eastern half is desert — three deserts, in fact: the Great Sandy Desert, the Gibson Desert and the Little Sandy Desert. Together they make up the Western Desert, a huge arid region reaching into the Northern Territory and South Australia. The desert is harsh but beautiful, with red sand rolling into the distance like huge waves, plains and rocky hillsides dotted with spinifex and salt lakes glittering in the blinding northern light. This is one of the hottest regions in the world, with summer temperatures topping forty degrees Celsius; only the deepest wells survive the hammering heat. Summer also brings the rains that turn dry riverbeds into raging torrents and transform the dusty plains into vast lakes and wetlands that attract great flocks of migratory birds.

Australian Heroines

For over 5000 years the Great Sandy Desert has been home to the Mardudjara people — the Mardu. Because of the scarcity of food in the desert, the Mardu were semi-nomadic, covering vast distances in their search for animals such as kangaroos, lizards, goannas, bush turkeys, small marsupials and witchetty grubs, as well as grass seeds, berries, nuts, honey and yams. On these long journeys, the Mardu carried fire sticks, hunting weapons, tools and *coolimans* (bark troughs for transporting food, water and babies).

White explorers reached the Pilbara in 1861 looking for grazing lands and, farther east, for an inland sea. They blazed the trail for sheep and cattle station owners, who began moving inexorably inland by the 1870s. To protect their flocks and herds, white settlers began fencing off vast tracts of land. Cut off from their tribal hunting grounds and facing starvation, the Aborigines fought back. In the hostilities that ensued, both Aborigines and whites were killed and injured.

To survive, the Aborigines began trickling out of the desert to settlements on the Canning Stock Route. The stock route consisted of a 14 000-kilometre track dotted with wells, which allowed drovers to herd cattle from Halls Creek in the Kimberley region to the south-eastern goldfields. Once Aboriginal hunting grounds, this land was now occupied by station owners. The relationship that developed between these Aborigines and the new settlers was, for the most part, friendly. The graziers needed workers, and the Aborigines needed security and a guaranteed supply of food and water. The tribal men became stockmen, and the women worked in the homesteads. The Aborigines had to learn to stay in one place for long periods and to wear hot, constricting clothes, but they held onto much of their traditional way of life. They kept up their tribal rituals and ceremonies, and went on hunting trips to supplement the white man's food.

Inevitably, the powerlessness of the Aborigines left them open to abuse. They were not paid for their work as stockmen, domestics and cooks. Even worse, many of the women were sexually exploited, some giving birth to part-Aboriginal children. As it was against the law in Western Australia for white men to marry Aboriginal women, these mothers had to bring up their children alone. Regarded as neither black nor white, the children were discriminated against by both races. They were called 'half-castes' or, insultingly, 'half-breeds' or 'mongrels'; the Aboriginal term for them was *muda-muda*.

The 'Stolen Children'

There is still considerable debate about whether or not such a thing as a 'stolen generation' of Aboriginal children exists. Aborigines maintain that hundreds of Aboriginal children were stolen from their parents over several decades by government authorities. Their opponents maintain that these children were not stolen, but removed by the state for their own welfare — either with the permission of their mothers (so they could be educated), or forcibly (because they were being neglected or mistreated or were considered uncontrollable). Others argue about how many children were taken, and when.

So, what do we mean by 'stolen children' and what was 'the stolen generation'?

The relationship between the Europeans who settled Australia in 1788 and the indigenous inhabitants was mainly friendly at first, but conflict soon broke out over land. When their hunting grounds were invaded, the Aborigines either had to move farther out into the countryside or stand and fight. Many chose to fight. In the battles that followed, there were casualties among both blacks and whites. As spears and waddies were no match for guns, the Aborigines, though they won many battles, could not win the war. Many ended up living in squalid camps on the edge of towns, victims of malnutrition, disease, alcohol, violence, and family and tribal breakdown.

Up until the 1850s, state governments sometimes removed Aboriginal children from their families in order to raise them as Christians and to educate them so they could get jobs as domestic and farm labourers.

By the middle of the nineteenth century the plight of the Aborigines was so appalling that Christian church leaders stepped in and convinced state governments to set aside land as Aboriginal reserves. Fearing that the Aboriginal race was dying out, the politicians agreed. With nowhere else to go, the Aborigines moved onto mission stations — reserves run by the churches — such as Point McLeay in South Australia from 1859, Maloga in Victoria from 1874, and Warangesda in New South Wales from 1879. This ushered in a period of peace and security for many Aborigines. On the missions, they were able to develop the skills necessary to survive in a white society and become self-sufficient. For the first time, they began to feel they were part of a larger group and developed a sense of belonging to the Aboriginal race rather than a family or a tribe.

As white settlers spread across the continent and more Aborigines came into contact with whites, the number of part-Aboriginal children increased rapidly. Instead of a dwindling Aboriginal population, as had been predicted, the number of people identifying themselves as Aborigines grew.

In the second half of the nineteenth century, state governments set up Boards for the Protection of the Aborigines, and appointed Chief Protectors of Aborigines — public servants with complete power over the lives of the Aborigines in their care. In Queensland and Western Australia, the Chief Protectors used their powers to force all indigenous people into large, highly-regulated government settlements and missions. By 1911 in all states the Chief Protector of Aborigines could have Aboriginal children removed by the police. Children on Aboriginal reserves were taken from their mothers at about the age of 4 and housed in dormitories away from their families. When they turned 14, they were sent away to work for white people. It also became illegal in some states for part-Aborigines to remain on the reserves or to receive government rations of food and clothing.

The idea behind this policy was to force part-Aboriginal people to 'blend' into white society through intermarriage with white people. The reality was very different, with many destitute Aborigines ending up in shanty towns on the fringes of country towns or near reserves.

In New South Wales, Western Australia and the Northern Territory, many part-Aboriginal children

Molly Craig

were removed from their families and placed in training institutions before being sent out to work. In New South Wales the children were sent to Aboriginal children's 'homes' at Cootamundra and Kinchela; in Victoria, they were sent to white child welfare institutions or adopted into white families. At Moore River in Western Australia, Colebrook in South Australia, the Half-Caste Institution in Alice Springs and Palm Island in Queensland, children were socialised into white society and their links with their own culture were broken. As well as being at risk of physical and sexual abuse, many never received wages for their labour. Often their names were changed, which made it difficult — if not impossible — for them to find their parents in later life. Perhaps one in three children were removed in the 1920s.

Meanwhile, farmers who wanted to use the valuable land for grazing forced governments to expel Aborigines from reserves. Some were moved from small, friendly reserves to larger reserves run by all-powerful managers. In Western Australia, hundreds of Aborigines were marched from fringe camps and reserves to the infamous Moore River Settlement, which at one point held 1300 people. Others tried to find refuge in fringe settlements on the outskirts of country towns, but were soon driven off by irate townsfolk.

At a conference in 1937, politicians and bureaucrats involved in Aboriginal welfare decided on a policy of 'assimilation' for part-Aborigines, whom they called 'half-castes'. This meant separating 'full-blood' and part-Aborigines and integrating part-Aboriginal children into white society. Large numbers of children were sent to institutions where they were given a primary school education, then sent out into the world to make their own way. From the 1940s onwards, Aboriginal children came under the same welfare laws as non-indigenous children. That meant they could be removed from their families for being 'neglected', 'destitute' or 'uncontrollable', rather than simply for being light-skinned.

In the 1950s and 1960s new ways of removing indigenous children were devised. They were adopted out at birth, or sent away to receive medical treatment or attend distant schools. To relieve the pressure on institutions, many were fostered out. These are the children the Aborigines call 'the stolen children' or 'the stolen generation'.

But though institutionalisation destroyed some Aborigines' racial identity, it turned others into activists. Stolen and removed children who returned to their communities took with them knowledge of how white society worked, and the skills necessary for dealing with the authorities. Many became community or national leaders — the late Charles Perkins, who

Molly Craig

became secretary of the Federal Department of Aboriginal Affairs in 1988 and, from 1994, chair of the Aboriginal and Torres Strait Islander Commission (ATSIC) was one, and Lowitja O'Donohoe, who also became chair of ATSIC, was another.

Aboriginal political activism began during the Great Depression of the 1930s, which hit the indigenous workers even harder than whites, as they were the first to lose their jobs. The Australian Aboriginal League was established in 1932, and on the 150th anniversary of white settlement in 1938, Aborigines held a Day of Mourning for what they had lost. World War II interrupted this fledgling protest movement, but it resurfaced in 1946, when two Aboriginal men and a white man organised a strike of Aboriginal cattlemen in the Pilbara in Western Australia. A number of Aborigines' Progress and Advancement Leagues were set up in the 1950s.

In the 1960s Australia underwent a cultural revolution. The country threw off many of its conservative views and people became more open and tolerant. Most of the pressure for change came from the young — the 'baby boomers', the generation born after the Second World War. Inspired by the African-American battle for civil rights being waged in the United States, both black and white Australians began to press for better treatment of the Aborigines. Until then, discrimination against

Aborigines had been enshrined in the law; they could not vote, were paid less than non-indigenous workers, and could not obtain social security benefits. The campaign was waged on two fronts: civil rights — the right of Aborigines to attend white schools, own property, buy land, drink in hotels and integrate into white society if they so chose — and reviving Aborigines' distinct cultural identity.

In 1966 about two hundred Gurindji people, including eighty station hands, walked off Wave Hill cattle station in the Northern Territory to protest against low wages and poor conditions, and began a fight to regain their tribal lands. This was the beginning of the battle for land rights.

Aboriginal activism and a groundswell of public opinion eventually led to the 1967 referendum on Aboriginal rights. In this national vote, Australians were asked if they wanted the Constitution amended to give the Commonwealth Government the power to make laws concerning Aborigines — until then the right of the state governments — and to enable Aborigines to be counted in the census, or population statistics.

Most Australians regarded the referendum as a vote on whether Aborigines should be given full citizenship rights, and 90.77 per cent voted yes. After the amendments were passed, the Holt Coalition Government set up a Council of Aboriginal Affairs and named a Minister for Aboriginal Affairs. The Australian Institute of Aboriginal Studies was established in 1968, and the Aboriginal Arts Board in 1973. By 1988 Aborigines had assumed control of regional management of their land councils, housing associations, co-operatives, cultural associations and child-care organisations. Link-Up, an organisation set up to put stolen children in touch with their relatives, was established and has helped many displaced children find their families.

The Hawke Labor Government of the 1980s accepted Aborigines' demands for self-determination and set up the Aboriginal and Torres Strait Islander Commission (ATSIC). It drew together the executive, advisory and policy-making functions of many government and non-government Aboriginal organisations. The Hawke Government also set up the Royal Commission into Aboriginal Deaths in Custody in 1987 in response to public outrage at the high death rate of Aborigines in jails.

In 1991 the Labor Government established a Council for Aboriginal Reconciliation. Its aims were to improve race relations, to foster national commitment to addressing Aboriginal and Torres Strait Islander peoples' social, economic and political disadvantage, and to encourage an appreciation of their cultures and achievements.

A significant advance in land rights occurred in

1992 when the High Court of Australia recognised that the people of the Murray Islands, in Torres Strait, held and continued to hold Native Title to their land. It found that Aboriginal title had not been extinguished by the European invasion, and that the Meriam people were entitled to possession, occupation, use and enjoyment of the Murray Islands. This was called the Mabo judgement, after Eddie Mabo, the man who brought the legal action with four other traditional owners. In 1993 the Federal Native Title Act was passed and tribunals were set up to hear land claims.

In 1994 a Bureau of Statistics report revealed that 10 per cent of Aboriginal and Torres Strait Islanders over 25 had been removed from their parents in childhood. Indigenous children are still six times more likely than non-indigenous children to be removed by child welfare authorities, and twenty-one times more likely to be placed in juvenile detention.

In 1995, acceding to pressure from Aborigines and their supporters, the Commonwealth Government finally mounted an inquiry into the question of the stolen children. Run by the Human Rights and Equal Opportunity Commission and headed by Sir Ronald Wilson, the inquiry was asked to trace past laws, practices and policies that resulted in the separation of indigenous children from their families by 'compulsion, duress or undue influence'.

Molly Craig

Its report, *Bringing them Home*, was released in May 1997. It stated that between one in three and one in ten indigenous children were forcibly removed from their families between 1910 and 1970, and that most Aboriginal and Torres Strait Islander families 'have been affected, in one or more generations, by the forcible removal of one or more children'. Describing assimilation policies as 'genocide', it called for compensation for Aborigines who had been removed from their families and for a national apology. Since then, some state governments, a variety of organisations and thousands of ordinary people have apologised for the wrongs that were done to Aboriginal Australians, but so far no national apology has been forthcoming. Aborigines continue to sue, unsuccessfully, for compensation through the courts.

Meanwhile, support for reconciliation continues to grow. On 28 May 2000 about 250 000 people marched across the Sydney Harbour Bridge to show their solidarity with the Aborigines and to say sorry for what has happened to them as a result of white settlement. Many thousands more marched in other states in the following weeks, and then in December 2000 over 300 000 marched in Melbourne.

Marika Cierer Weinberger

Holocaust Survivor

Marika and Edita Cierer in 1940. Photo courtesy Marika Weinberger.

Marika Cierer Weinberger

In June 1944, when Germany had almost lost the war, the Nazis swooped on Hungary's Jews. Fifteen-year-old Marika Cierer was transported to Auschwitz, the infamous German concentration camp in Poland, with her two grandmothers, her parents, her aunt Olga and her older sister, Edita. For a year, Marika, Olga and Edita were imprisoned, starved, beaten and worked to the brink of death. But they survived, and were liberated by the Russians in August 1945.

Born in 1928, Eva Marianna 'Marika' Cierer lived a comfortable life in the town of Zilina in the west of Slovakia, one of the provinces of Czechoslovakia. Hers was a close-knit Jewish family. Her father, Vojtech Cierer, had a senior position with an insurance company. Her mother, Irena, looked after the family and their spacious, modern apartment. Marika was a good student, who enjoyed sports such as ice-skating, skiing, fencing and swimming. In the summer holidays, while her parents travelled, she and her sister Edita would return to their parents' home town of Kosice — south-east of Zilina and near the border of Hungary — and stay with

The Cierer family in 1933. l to r: Irena, Edita, Marika and Vojtech.
Photo courtesy Marika Weinberger.

their grandmothers. Both Marika and Edita, who was seven years older, had plans to study medicine.

But outside Czechoslovakia, war was looming. By 1939, Slovakia had become a puppet state of Germany, run by local Nazis. Marika was 11 and Edita 18 when Zilina became part of the German Reich. Following in the footsteps of their German masters, the new government immediately excluded Jews from most professions and locked their children out of the state schools. Edita was allowed to finish her final year of high school, but the girls' happy, secure childhood had come to an end.

Marika's parents read the danger signs and decided to leave Slovakia. They considered moving to London to start over again, but eventually decided to return to their family in Kosice, which had been taken over by Hungary in 1938 and renamed Kassa. It seemed like a safe haven. Although the Hungarian government had always been anti-Semitic and was prepared to make life difficult for its Jewish citizens, it was still resisting Nazi pressure to send them to concentration camps. Then on 3 September 1939, after Hitler had invaded Poland, Britain and France declared war on Germany. World War II had begun.

In Kassa, Marika was unaware of Hitler's plan to kill all the Jews in Europe. She had her own problems — the most pressing was learning enough Hungarian to start high school. But by the start of the new term, she again found herself locked out of the state school. Determined to give her the best possible education, Marika's parents found a Catholic school that would take her — at a price. The small group of Jewish girls accepted by the school had to pay double for school fees and extras like going to the theatre. They were also expected to attend Christian chapel every morning. 'We were handled differently and talked to differently,' recalls Marika. 'We were allowed to join the school, but were treated as second-class citizens.'

The net of anti-Semitism cast across Europe continued to tighten around the Cierer family. After years of service, Vojtech Cierer was sacked from his job with the insurance company. To keep food on the table, he went into business as a silent partner with a non-Jewish businessman selling wine and spirits. Somehow, he and Irena found the money for Marika's English tutor and French lessons at the *Alliance Française*. After school, she took Hebrew and Jewish studies with an unemployed Jewish professor. The outbreak of war and the quotas placed on Jews in the universities had put an end to Edita's dream of studying medicine; she was apprenticed to a dressmaker so she could earn a living.

In 1941 the Hungarian government passed a law requiring its one million Jews to prove that they were citizens. Those who failed would be 'resettled' in the eastern part of the German Reich. Unfortunately for Irena Cierer's family, her father, Josef Aschheim, had never taken out citizenship, even though he'd lived in Hungary since he was 3 years old. In August 1941, 22 000 Jews were taken from areas occupied by Hungary. In this round-up, nine members of the Aschheim family — four uncles, three aunts and two cousins — were loaded onto trains and taken away, ostensibly to work camps in the east. They were never seen again. Of Irena's family, only her mother, Grandmother Irma, and her sister, Aunt Olga, remained. The Holocaust, which had already swept away millions of European Jews, had finally caught up with the Cierer family.

Fortunately, Marika's father had seen what was coming and bought false papers for his family.

The Jews of Kassa tried to remain optimistic, hoping that the Allies would win the war before Hitler moved on Hungary. But Marika's father, who listened to the BBC news from London on his clandestine radio every day, feared that things were going to get much worse before they got better. He was right. In 1942 the Nazi High Command began to implement the infamous 'final solution', Hitler's plan to exterminate all the Jews of Europe.

During 1942 Vojtech Cierer was forced to spend time in labour camps. With no money coming in, Irena began selling off jewellery and valuables. Then the Catholic Church caved in to government pressure and expelled its Jewish students. With four years of high school still in front of her, Marika had to try to find a Jewish school that would take her. But these schools were all in other towns, which would mean leaving home. When her best friend, Judy Bergida, went off to study in Budapest, Marika was torn, but eventually decided not to go with her. She knew how badly her mother needed her after the loss of her own brothers and sisters. 'I felt selfish wanting to go,' she says. Instead, she joined a study group taught by a family of Jewish teachers who were no longer allowed to work, and became a private, or external student at the Ungvar Hebrew Gymnasium.

Every couple of months her father would take her to Ungvar on the overnight train for special tuition or exams.

Marika's life began to get her down. 'Instead of young teenagers, we were little old people,' she recalls. 'There were so many rules for Jewish people: don't do this, don't go there, say this, be careful.' To keep their spirits up, Vojtech took Marika and Edita to Budapest, where they saw four plays in four nights. As Marika was mad about the theatre, the outing gave her a new lease of life. But then, on 19 March 1944, the German army marched into Hungary. 'I'll always remember that day,' says Marika. 'There was a festival on. We were having an afternoon tea dance and a little play in the orphanage where we did volunteer work. I recited poetry. My parents were there. Everybody was having a nice time. My father was called away to the phone and came back looking pale. "Is something wrong?" I asked. He said it was just a call from a friend in Budapest.

'When it was time to go home, at about six or seven o'clock, we begged to be able to stay. My father said, "Yes, go on. Have a good time." Afterwards we walked home as a family and went to bed. Father was very quiet. I knew it was because of the phone call, but I thought, "I won't ask".'

In the middle of the night Marika woke to find her father standing at the open window in her

Marika Cierer Weinberger

Marika Cierer (right) with her best friend Judy Bergida and Zoli Reich from the play at the orphanage on 19 March 1944, the day the Germans marched into Hungary. Photo courtesy Marika Weinberger.

bedroom. 'What are you doing?' she asked. 'They've caught up with us,' he said. 'Come here.' The words chilled Marika. She went to the window and saw squads of German soldiers goose-stepping down the street. The clatter of boots on the cobble-stones had woken her father. Soon after, Irena and Edita joined them in Marika's room. No one uttered a word.

Determined to exterminate as many Jews as possible before the war ended, the Germans moved with terrifying speed and efficiency. In just seven weeks they would transport half a million Jews from the Hungarian countryside to Auschwitz. 'From

20 March to 3 June something happened every minute, each more unpleasant than the last,' says Marika. 'It started with having to wear a yellow star and finished with being herded onto trains and deported.'

The Germans began rounding up Jewish citizens and holding them for ransom. Henrik Cierer — Vojtech's younger brother — fled to Slovakia, followed by his wife and two children. Marika's tiny 79-year-old grandmother, Omama Cierer, saved her sons, Peter and Vojtech, when the gendarmes came to pick them up. Omama, who had fled anti-Semitic pogroms in Poland as a young woman, knew how to deal with the police. She told them Peter and Vojtech had abandoned her; they were bad sons.

To avoid capture, Vojtech began sleeping on a sofa in the office of Konrad Glatz, the family solicitor and a Gentile, or non-Jew. Irena told the police he was in a labour camp somewhere. Soon Peter Cierer's house was confiscated, and his family of five squeezed in with Vojtech's. A curfew was imposed on Jews, keeping them indoors from 6 p.m. till 10 a.m. One day, when Irena broke the curfew by a few minutes to get to the markets, their next door neighbour spat on her. Marika was devastated. 'I realised that, if the man next door could do such a thing, this town was not somewhere I could build a life. That I carried in me.'

Next, the Nazis began moving all the Jews into a ghetto, or closed quarter. Grandmother Irma Aschheim had to stand by as strangers invaded her house. Grandmother Cierer, Omama, joined her son Peter and his family in Vojtech's house.

At Easter 1944 the Cierers celebrated Passover as usual. 'Here we were packing up to move into the ghetto and praying at the same time,' says Marika. She wondered how God could allow this. Then came the long-dreaded knock on the door. 'All right, Jews!' barked the Hungarian police. 'It's time to go! First put all your jewellery and money on the table.' The gendarmes even took her parents' wedding rings and Edita's baby earrings. 'They ripped them out of her ears. She was bleeding.' However, they managed to keep the rings Edita had sewn into the padded shoulders of their clothes.

Carrying 50 kilograms each — blankets, food, bedding, pillows and cooking utensils — Marika's family were marched to their new home. It was a tiny studio flat — one room with couches for beds, and an electric hot plate in the bathroom for cooking — but they were relieved to be together still. In the meantime, the Germans swept through nearby towns and villages rounding up Jews, who they housed initially in private homes, schools and synagogues in Kassa. The Cierers tried to help these bewildered refugees. 'We thought, us next. It was the beginning of the end.'

After herding the country Jews into the town brickyard, where they were assembling people for deportation, the Germans began moving them out on trains in April 1944. As the brickyard emptied out, Jews from the ghetto were brought in. Realising their turn would come soon, Vojtech sat the family down for a serious discussion. He told them he'd left valuables with his solicitor Konrad Glatz, who had also offered to get them Christian papers and put them on the midnight train to Budapest. 'I think you girls should go,' Vojtech said. Fifteen-year-old Marika was thrown into confusion. When she told Edita, who was now 22, that she did not want to go, her sister decided to stay with her. 'I didn't want to leave my parents to their fate,' Marika says. 'And to be honest, I was frightened. I'll never know if Edita would have gone. I think she would have. In the camp I used to think, "What have I done to this woman?" I'm sure my sister would have managed to stay free on the outside.' Their mother was relieved, but their father was disappointed.

As May drew to a close it was the Cierers' turn to enter the brickyard. This humiliating march through her hometown is one of Marika's most painful memories of the war. 'They lined us up and we started to shuffle through town. Lots of neighbours and friends, even some of my old school friends, were lining the street. They were laughing and making remarks about us. I wondered, "Did we ever have friends here?" I suppose the decent people didn't come out. I lost any faith and belief in human nature that day. I thought, "The world has gone crazy".'

At the brickyard they were reunited with the grandmothers and Marika's friend Judy Bergida, who had returned from Budapest, and her mother. The brickyard was primitive — open at the sides, it was cavernous and cold. The latrines stank, and they had to sleep on mattresses on the floor and line up for food. But people were still hopeful. They tried to make their little spaces comfortable, and the teenagers sang and gossiped. Marika and Judy talked endlessly about what they would do after the war, when they returned home. On Friday night they lit candles to celebrate Shabbat, the Jewish Sabbath, put on their best clothes, and promenaded and chatted with friends. Some young couples even celebrated their weddings in the brickyard.

Over the next few days, the brickyard became a ghost town as more and more trains filled up and steamed out. 'We said, "Goodbye, see you there". But where? We thought wherever we were going couldn't be much worse than here.' One of the train drivers advised them to leave their suitcases behind. The luggage would make the carriage unbearably crowded, he warned, and would only be confiscated at the other end. Thinking he wanted to steal their belongings, they refused to listen. But when patients from the hospital — among them Aunty Olga, who had broken her ankle — and inmates from the mental hospital and the jail were brought in, fear swept through the brickyard. 'It was a spring cleaning,' says Marika. 'They even brought in Jewish babies that the nuns had been hiding in the Catholic hospital. When they brought the babies, my father realised what was happening.'

Then, finally, it was their turn. On Friday 2 June, wearing several layers of their best clothes and taking the last of their good food, the Cierers were locked into a wagon with their carefully labelled suitcases. After midnight on 3 June, the final transport, Number 4, pulled out in the pouring rain. On it were the last of the Jews of Kassa. In the chaos, Marika became separated from her family and panicked until her father found her.

Seventy-five people were crammed into each carriage of the cattle truck. Because the luggage took up so much space, most of the men had to stand. The fear was palpable. Babies began to scream, but when their parents slung them from the ceilings in hammocks, the rocking of the train quieted them. To this day, Marika cannot stand the sound of babies crying. Buckets served as lavatories, and privacy was impossible. Very little air or light could penetrate the small, barred windows. 'The lack of oxygen played tricks on the mind,' says Marika. 'Although I was within touching distance of my family, I felt I was miles away.' The food soon ran out, but it was thirst that drove people mad. Desperate, they opened bottles of pickles and tins and drank the liquid. 'It was the journey to hell,' recalls Marika. 'You could not imagine the look, the sound, the smells of that train. It's not possible to get rid of the smell of filth and the hunger and thirst from my memory. I thought, "Dear God, let me survive this experience and maybe the next one will be easier".'

All the while, guards from the feared *Schutz-Staffel* or SS — the special police force which had the task of exterminating Jews — ranged though the carriages demanding silk stockings, clothes and jewellery. Bit by bit the Cierer family lost their clothes and valuables. Fortunately, Stephen Grunstein, who was like an older brother to Marika, was standing nearby. He calmed her down and tried to keep her spirits up.

Several hours into the journey, the train turned east. It was then that many of the adults realised they could not be going to a labour camp in Slovakia. Having heard rumours about death camps in Poland, they feared the worst. Their fears were justified. On Sunday 4 June 1944, only two days before the Allies landed at Normandy to liberate Europe, the last train from Kassa reached its destination — Auschwitz, a name that has become synonymous with horror and inhumanity.

When the train doors crashed open, the dazed and exhausted travellers tumbled out into a nightmare. In front of them was a giant set of gates bearing the words *Arbeit Macht Frei* — work will set you free. At the railway siding, hunched people in strange pyjama-like uniforms rushed to and fro; SS guards screamed orders; dogs barked. 'What kind of madhouse is this?' wondered Marika, almost paralysed with shock. 'Who are these strange people in uniforms with numbers on them? Mad people? Criminals?'

First, the Germans separated the men and women. Nobody resisted. 'We were beginning to understand that we were here to take orders, that we had no choice,' says Marika. Edita and Marika lined up beside their Aunty Olga, who now walked with a stick. Irena and the two grandmothers were behind them, and Vojtech was nearby in the men's line. The girls panicked when his line suddenly marched away, but it quickly returned. On that short walk Vojtech Cierer realised what lay in store for them. When Marika asked him if they would be able to stay together, he said, 'Not always.' 'What do you mean?' Marika asked. Her father only said, 'Edita, look after the child.'

'That frightened me,' says Marika. 'I was uneasy,

but I thought maybe we'd be separated and meet up again later. Then they marched my father away again. That was the last time I saw him.'

Meanwhile, men in striped pyjamas and caps ran up and down between the line of women and the train, unloading luggage. One stopped beside Marika for a second. Taking his life in his hands, he asked in Yiddish, 'How old are you?' Startled, Marika replied: 'Fifteen'. 'No, you are 18!' he said, and ran off. On his next trip he grabbed Olga's walking stick and threw it under the train. Then he hissed at Marika: 'Put your head down, The Dog is here!'

The Dog was the inmates' name for Dr Josef Mengele, also known as the Angel of Death. Mengele, a medical doctor attached to the camp, occasionally came to the station to pick out specimens for his research. He particularly liked people who were genetically unusual, like twins and dwarfs. He subjected them to horrifying medical experiments, often without anaesthetic: they were injected with poisons and bacteria; had limbs amputated and organs removed; were immersed in freezing water to see how long they could survive; and had chemicals and poisons dripped into their eyes to test the effects. With her dark hair, light skin and huge blue eyes, Marika could easily have attracted Mengele's interest.

Edita was the first to front Mengele and the other

SS officers. He signalled her to the left. Next came Olga, who managed to trot despite her ankle. When it was Marika's turn, Mengele looked her over. 'How old are you?' he asked. Marika did not hesitate. 'Eighteen,' she said, keeping her eyes cast down. She was tall enough to get away with it. Signalled to the left, she ran to her sister and aunt. She'd had a narrow escape. The Nazis kept only strong, healthy men and women who could work hard on very little food and sleep. Children and teenagers were usually sent straight to the gas chambers. Looking back, Marika saw her mother and grandmothers in the line to the right. The Germans called this inhuman cull the selection.

This first 'selection' stands out in Marika's mind as if it happened yesterday. 'I can still smell the wagons and feel the sun and the cold together on my skin and feel the exhaustion.' Then they were marched into Auschwitz. 'There were thousands and thousands of people in striped uniforms behind barbed wire, women on one side, some in grey dresses, some in stripes,' recalls Marika. 'None had hair.' These scarecrows screamed at them in Yiddish, Slovakian and Hungarian: 'Throw us your clothes! They'll only take them anyway!' But by now the new arrivals had only one outfit and their shoes left. To Marika, the prisoners looked deranged. 'I thought, "This will never happen to us".'

Forced on at a trot by barking dogs and screaming SS guards, they passed thousands of men shuffling along in complete silence. Ahead were rows of huts, a city of barracks. Marika thought: 'Is that where they live? It can't be.'

Uniformed women with guns patrolled the line shouting orders. Marika soon discovered that these female guards, who had been criminals or prostitutes before the war, were even more cruel than the men. 'Giving that extra hiding seemed to give them deep pleasure,' she says.

'Halt!' barked a voice, and they stopped in the midst of a sea of barracks. This was Birkenau, the women's prison at Auschwitz. Tired and thirsty, they were forced to undress in front of male guards with dogs. Clad only in her shoes, Marika had her plaits cut off, then a male barber shaved her head and body. She was mortified. 'In those days you didn't even undress in front of your mother. I felt as if the whole world had turned upside down, but I couldn't ask any questions. We didn't talk, Aunty Olga, Edita and I. There was nothing to say.'

Then came the saga of the shoes. Marika had put on her skating boots for the journey. They were light and strong, but dirty. Unfortunately, Edita was wearing shiny boots. An SS woman decided she wanted them. But when she ordered Edita to take them off, Edita refused. 'Do it!' ordered the woman.

'No!' said Edita, who still believed she was in the real world. Enraged, the guard called two female prisoners, who wrenched off Edita's boots and socks. As punishment, the guard threw her one large man's shoe and one woman's high-heeled shoe. Edita had to hobble around in these ridiculous and uncomfortable shoes for months before she was issued wooden clogs. 'She marched for miles every day in those shoes,' says Marika. 'For the rest of her life she walked a bit funny. That little game cost her dearly.'

With dusk coming on it was getting chilly. Still the women waited outside, naked and shivering. They could not be fitted into the crowded camp until some of the inmates were moved out, usually to the gas chambers. They spent the night in the washroom, a huge, cold concrete barrack with wash troughs and dripping taps. Young nursing mothers, who'd had their babies wrenched from them, moaned in agony from the pain in their breasts. Women shivered and cried.

And still they'd been given nothing to drink. When they asked for water, they were told they weren't at a holiday resort. For fun, the guards brought in buckets of water and threw them over the women. 'If you remained sane that night, it was another miracle,' says Marika. She and her aunt and sister huddled together to stay warm. Others died of cold during the night.

The next morning, still naked, they were ushered

out into the cold grey dawn and lined up to be counted. This was to be their first experience of the dreaded *Appel*, or headcount. The Germans obsessively counted the prisoners in their camps three times a day, often keeping them standing for hours till they got the tally right. Those who collapsed or died in the barracks had to be dragged into the line to be counted. Others fell dead during the *Appel*. Half-dead from exhaustion and thirst, Marika thought: 'If this is not the end, it should be. We can't go much lower.'

In an attempt to stop herself from going mad, she fixed on a group of women in the distance, and convinced herself that one of them was her mother. But as she watched, the guards set the dogs on the woman, who was torn to pieces. Horrified, Marika tried to reassure herself that it wasn't her mother, just an hallucination. Later she would drive Edita mad by insisting her father must be among the men they saw in the camps they passed through.

After two more days spent standing around, the women were given thin, scratchy grey summer uniforms and wooden clogs. Because nobody wanted them, Marika was able to keep her skating boots. Eventually, a barrack became vacant, and a thousand women were herded into a long empty room with bare concrete floors; there was nowhere to sit, nowhere to sleep. Every day at 5.00 a.m., at noon and again in the evening, they were trotted out to line up for the interminable *Appels*.

The air was grey and greasy and a terrible stench of burning hung over the camp. When Marika asked one of the long-term residents where her parents could be, the woman said: 'Look up there. See the chimney? That's where they are.' But the idea of bodies being burned in huge ovens was unthinkable. 'Nobody believed it,' says Marika. 'I would not have dared to think it.'

After less than a week in Birkenau, Marika, Edita and Olga were loaded onto trains with about a thousand other women and moved out again with only the clothes they stood up in. Nobody dared to ask where they were going. To sustain them on the long journey, they were given only a piece of bread and margarine. It was not enough. In Birkenau, Marika had subsisted on heavy black bread and a piece of sausage. She'd refused the thin, evil-smelling soup, but now she longed for it.

After an endless journey, they reached Riga, the capital of the Baltic state of Latvia. They were so far north that the sun shone twenty-four hours a day in summer. With the citizens of Riga jeering from windows and footpaths, they were marched through the city to Kaiserwald camp. Marika was distraught: how would her parents ever find her here?

Despite the usual screaming guards and hysterical

dogs, Kaiserwald was very different from Auschwitz. It was smaller, and nobody went naked. The Latvian Jewish women who already occupied the barracks had long hair and their own clothes and make-up. The Latvians were not pleased to see them. 'They treated us as enemies,' says Marika. 'Whatever we did was wrong. They made us feel we didn't belong there. They believed that because we had our hair cut off, and because we had lice, we must be Hungarian Gypsies.' Olga, Edita, Marika, and Judy Bergida and her mother managed to stay together. By now, Marika and Judy had realised they would be lucky to come out of this alive. Marika says: 'We used to sit and talk after a work shift and Judy would say, "You will survive Marika. You have to survive to tell people what happened to us".'

When it came time to be allocated to work groups, or *Kommandos*, they were separated. Marika was lucky enough to be put to work in the vegetable garden, but she did not keep the job for long. Raised in towns, she had never tended a garden before. 'I pulled out vegetables instead of weeds. I got a huge beating and was thrown out. The guards pushed me, beating me and screaming all the way, to a factory where my aunt and sister were working.'

It was a munitions factory. For twelve hours a day Marika worked on an assembly line manufacturing small components — what they were she never discovered. It was eye-glazing and gruelling, but at least she was among friends. Soon the Russians began bombing the factory, however, and the workers were redeployed. The next job was much harder. Every morning they set out from the camp at 4.30 a.m. to walk to the airport several kilometres away — Edita in her odd shoes, Olga with her broken ankle (which refused to heal), and Marika, held up by her sister and aunt. 'I used to sleepwalk and dream about food,' says Marika. 'Sleepiness was my biggest enemy — and the cold. I never had enough sleep.'

From 6.00 a.m. till 6.00 p.m. the women did heavy construction work with pneumatic drills. For a half-starved child, it was torture. After two weeks, Marika's health started to fail, and pus-filled, weeping sores erupted on her arms and legs. Knowing how bad she looked, Marika dreaded the daily selections, where the guards culled the sick and weak. Those who failed were taken away in trucks. That was why the Latvian women wore make-up, Marika realised — to look healthy. Those who didn't have lipstick or rouge bit their lips and pinched their cheeks to put some colour in their faces. Aware that her sores were a death sentence, Marika covered them up with her long uniform and high boots, but eventually the pain of lacing up her boots became unbearable.

One day Marika gave up. She simply could not lace up her boots for the selection. Edita said,

'I'm going to do up your shoes.' 'No, I'll die,' said Marika. 'Here, put this rag in your mouth and bite down while I do up your shoes,' Edita ordered. Obediently Marika lay down on the bed and screamed silently into her gag while her sister laced up her boots. Then came the march to the *Appel*. When she saw Marika hobbling, Edita hissed, 'Walk properly.' 'I can't!' said Marika. But she did. 'I stood there in agony,' she recalls. 'The pain was worse than childbirth. The guard looked at me and said, "Laufen!" ("Run!") and somehow I did.' As soon as she was safe, she passed out.

With the Russians approaching, the guards held a special selection to clear out the camp. Judy and her mother were taken that day. The shock was too much for Marika; she refused to accept that her friends were going to their deaths, that she would never see them again. Kaiserwald was evacuated on 2 August 1944. On the forced march to the Vistula River, where barges were waiting to ferry them to another camp, Marika was only semi-conscious. Half-carried by her aunt and sister, she passed out several times. In the dark and smelly hold of the barge, she developed diarrhoea. Fortunately, Joly Atlas, the mother of another friend called Judy, looked after her. Joly covered her with a scrap of blanket and scrounged a few mouthfuls of foul, petrol-tasting water. But it was enough; miraculously, Marika settled down. Through her fog and pain she heard an SS guard asking if the girl was still alive. Joly begged him to leave her alone.

Though Marika was still alive when the barge docked in Danzig, now Gdansk in Poland, she could not move fast enough for the guards. Enraged, one of them hit her in the face with the butt of his rifle to hurry her along. She found out later that he had broken her cheekbone. Face on fire, head aching and half-delirious, Marika shuffled into Stutthof, a women's transit camp. She soon found out what sort of place this was. One of the guards purposely spilt scalding soup on Edita's arm. Handing them each a dish, he told them to look after it, as they would have to use it for everything.

At Stutthof, a thousand women were crammed into a barrack that could comfortably hold only about five hundred. Wedged up against a wall under a locked window, Marika realised what the guard had meant: if she wanted to relieve herself in the night, she would have to use her food dish. A Polish guard called Barbara, who boasted that she had killed her own mother, was in charge. To amuse herself, Barbara threw a few crusts of bread into the crowd and laughed as the starving women trampled each other to death. Marika watched in horror. The next night a barrack with bunks became available, and it was here, on 7 August 1944, that Marika celebrated her sixteenth birthday. She had forgotten about it, but the others had not. Joly Atlas gave her a little 'birthday cake' made of bread. 'She was a second mother to me,' says Marika. The memory of that gift still makes her weep.

In mid-September, filthy, starving and lice-ridden, they were on the move again. In Stutthof they'd been given civilian clothes, and Marika was wearing a ridiculous maroon cocktail gown with a lace collar. Doubtless its owner was long dead. This time the train took them to Glöwen, a satellite of Sachsenhausen concentration camp outside Berlin. This was regarded as good luck. Glöwen was small, and the Commandant was not a sadistic madman. The *Kapos*, or prison trusties, were chosen from among the women themselves, and the discipline was not as severe as that at other camps. Best of all, there were no selections. On Sundays they were allowed to take a shower, and clean up. This meant picking lice off their clothes and bodies and shaking out their straw mattresses.

They were assigned to barracks housing a hundred women, given striped uniforms and a white headscarf, and put to work the next morning. For the first time Marika was separated from her sister and aunt: they were in different barracks and on different work *Kommandos*. The work varied. During one of Europe's coldest winters on record, she might one day be sitting down working in a factory; a week later she could be wrestling with a pneumatic drill or helping other girls push a trainload of coal in temperatures of twenty degrees below zero.

By this time Marika was a physical wreck. She developed meningitis, and her sores had run riot. A Romanian Jewish doctor at the camp hospital treated her sores, but when Edita heard that people who spent too much time in hospital were being taken away by truck, she stopped Marika going. After that, the doctor treated her secretly late at night. Then she contracted diphtheria. Her temperature soared to forty degrees and she could not swallow. The doctor saved her life by forcing open her throat and swabbing it out with cotton buds made from toothpicks. She survived.

Outside, the tide was turning against the Nazis — they were losing the war. The Allies were bombing Germany, and the camp was caught in a pincer movement between the Russians and the Americans. When the bombers thundered overhead, the guards locked the prisoners in their barracks and ran away to hide. Despite the danger, the women were ecstatic. 'The sky was rocking. We were clapping. The guards were terrified,' recalls Marika. Suddenly, the SS women began behaving nicely: they were frightened they might be called to account after the war.

In Glöwen, Edita had a prized job in the warm camp laundry, but Marika was still being sent out on work *Kommandos*. To keep her little sister alive, Edita wrapped one of their blankets — they had two each, and slept together with one under them and three on top — around her body and smuggled it to the laundry, where she cut it up and turned it into a warm jacket. This was a serious matter — defacing German property was an offence punishable by death. One day, Marika forgot to take the jacket off when she left for work. When she returned that night, the Camp Commandant was at the gate. 'I thought, "I'm finished; I'm dead."' But the German only felt the jacket, asked 'How many blankets does it take to make such a nice jacket?', and let her pass. She almost fainted with relief.

By April it was clear that the war was coming to an end. But still the Germans would not let their Jewish prisoners go. Every day the guards reminded their captives that there was still time to finish them off.

When the fighting got too close, work stopped. The Germans abandoned the camp and set off, driving the prisoners ahead of them. Marika, Edita, Olga and their friends, who now included two Hungarian girls, Babette and Margaret, were very weak and had diarrhoea. They worried about their capacity to survive another march, even though their destination, Ravensbrück, wasn't far away. The journey was difficult and dangerous. It was snowing, bombs were raining down, and the roads were crammed with fleeing refugees, soldiers, burnt-out vehicles, debris and dead horses. Russian planes, flying so low Marika could see the pilots' faces, strafed anything that moved. The guards shot anyone who fell behind or stopped to defecate. Nearly at the end of her physical and emotional limits, Marika just wanted to lie down and find peace. To keep her going, Edita threatened, 'If you sit down, I'll shoot you.' It was the thought of her parents that kept Marika going. Though she knew in her heart that her mother was probably dead, she believed her father might survive. How would he feel if she didn't return?

Eventually they reached Ravensbrück in one piece. The most infamous of the women's camps, it had turned into a madhouse, full of Gypsies, Seventh Day Adventists, Jews from the last transports out of Hungary, and fierce women who fought each other with knives. Marika, who'd seen these women carving up dead horses on the road and fighting over the carcasses, was terrified of them. 'I thought it would be strange to be killed by one of these women with a knife after surviving all this time,' she says.

With the Russians closing in, discipline had broken down at the camp. There was no room for the new arrivals in the barracks, and the Germans were too busy packing the loot they'd stolen from the prisoners to hold *Appels*. But still they would not let the Jews go free. Ordering them to leave everything behind, the guards herded them onto trains, locked them in overnight, then unloaded them again, lined them back up and marched them out to Malchov camp. This was little more than a death march for many. For Edita and Olga it was the last straw, and this time it was up to Marika to keep them going. She even carried Edita on her back some of the way. But there was one light moment on this trek. One night, when they were lying exhausted on the road, Margaret said to Marika: 'When we get out of here, I have the perfect boy for you.' After that, everyone teased Marika about her future 'husband'.

On 1 May 1945 the ragged band reached Malchov. Told to sit down, they collapsed on the ground. Snooping around the camp the next day, Marika thought she could smell soup. She feared she might be hallucinating, but when she crawled towards the scent she came upon big cauldrons of hot soup, sitting unattended. It was then she realised that all the Germans had left. Even so, she didn't dare take any soup without permission. She crawled back to her family and said: 'The gates are open! The Germans have gone!' Edita roused herself and scoffed, 'You're crazy, Marika.' 'No, I'm not. Look around. There are no guards here.' Instead of being glad, though, Marika was worried. 'Who'll give us the soup?' she wailed.

Rumours that the war had ended raced through

the camp. Not knowing what to do, everyone waited. The following day, 2 May, the first Russian soldier rode in on a horse. Ecstatic, the women leapt up and jumped around him. His horror at the sight of the filthy, ragged skeletons showed on his face. 'He was my mirror,' says Marika. 'He made me realise what we looked like.' A tall, healthy girl of 56 kilograms barely a year before, Marika now weighed about 40 kilograms. Then some Russian women soldiers arrived. The inmates were liberated, but to what? 'It wasn't possible for us to jump around and sing and dance because the war had ended,' says Marika. 'We were traumatised, finished, and we had nowhere to go.'

The Russians doled out the soup the guards had left behind, and opened up the store-rooms. They thought they were being kind. 'There was plenty of food in there, even boxes from the Red Cross that had never been distributed,' says Marika. 'People were opening sacks of sugar and lying in it and stuffing it in their mouths. The Russians didn't know enough to stop them.' People who had survived years of deprivation now died from overeating.

Marika only fully realized it was over a few weeks later, when the Czech government sent private cars and trucks to pick them up. The women were given food and clothing and driven to Prague. 'The reception in Prague stands out in my memory,' recalls Marika. 'A vast proportion of the population were standing in the streets to welcome us back. There was bread, cakes, singing. I finally felt free and back home. Or so I thought.'

The women made their way to Bratislava, the capital of Slovakia, to look for their family. They found Stephen Grunstein, who'd comforted Marika on the train to Auschwitz. He'd been with her father in the camp, but did not tell them what had become of him. Thirty years later, while visiting Stephen in Israel, Marika learned that Vojtech had been taken from Auschwitz to Hirschberg camp. He'd been there until October 1944, when he'd become ill and had been removed to Dachau in Germany, where he was killed. There was never any proof of the fate of Irena, who had almost certainly gone straight to the gas chambers in Auschwitz with Omama and Grandmother Irma.

The girls hopped trains to Kosice with Stephen. They found Uncle Peter living alone in his old house — his wife and children had perished. Strangers were living in Omama's house; Edita tried to get it back, but Marika only wanted to get away. They learned that Uncle Henrik had made it to Slovakia, but had been turned in to the police in Bratislava and transported to Oranienberg at Sachsenhausen. Later they received a letter from a Swedish doctor telling them that Henrik had accompanied a shipload of tuberculosis patients from Oranienberg to Sweden after liberation, but had died of TB on the way. He is buried in Sweden, but the family have never been able to find his grave. After the war Marika also learned that her uncles, aunts and cousins had not been 'resettled' in 1941, but taken to Ukraine, lined up on the banks of the Dnestr River and shot.

Marika's friends, Margaret and Babette, returned to Hungary. But Margaret turned up in Kosice suddenly one night to tell Marika she'd found 'the boy'. 'I said, "She's mad, don't let her in",' recalls Marika. But because Margaret's family ran a food-importing business and had plenty to eat, Marika went back to Hungary with her. There she met 'the boy', Alex Weinberger, who had been interned in labour camps when he turned eighteen and liberated early in 1945. For Marika's seventeenth birthday, he presented her with seventeen red roses. They were married in 1946.

The young couple now had to decide where to live. Marika no longer felt welcome in Kosice, where only 450 Jews had survived out of 12 000. Nor would she set foot in a German displaced persons camp. 'I thought we had to go somewhere where we could battle for ourselves,' she says. Some Jews illegally entered Palestine, which was then controlled by the British, but Marika could not bear the thought of being a fugitive again.

In the end, the young couple followed Alex's two

brothers to Paris. The French were turning a blind eye to Jewish refugees entering the country, but would not give them work permits. However, the three Weinberger brothers all found jobs, Alex with a Jewish newspaper, and their sister Manci joined them. By this time Marika was pregnant. After the trauma and the upheavals of the war, she was happy to stay at home, taking care of the house and cooking in their cramped hotel room. 'I was not ready to go out into the world,' she says. When Alex's older brother Harry decided to go to Palestine — soon to become Israel — Marika held out. She did not want Alex to do the compulsory military service. 'We'd sacrificed so much, and lost so many. I thought, "No more".'

As Marika's sister-in-law Manci had friends in Australia, the Weinberger family decided to come here. 'I didn't know what to expect,' says Marika. 'If I couldn't or wouldn't go to Israel, Australia was an excellent choice. It was perfect for healing. The people were welcoming and quietly understanding. We had wonderful neighbours. They didn't ask any questions.'

Alex and Marika followed Manci to Brisbane in 1950, and became Australian citizens in 1956. 'If I were to nominate my day of liberation, it would perhaps be that evening in Brisbane Town Hall when I finally became a full citizen of Australia with full rights. All our neighbours came and stood up and clapped. We got home and found they'd organised a surprise party.'

Having given up on the idea of becoming a rabbi, Alex went into business with his younger brother George in a furniture factory, which grew into a shop and showroom. In 1958 Alex was appointed Executive Director of the Jewish National Fund in Melbourne, then in 1963 Alex, Marika and their two daughters moved to Sydney, where they ran a boutique in Double Bay. That same year, Edita and her husband came to Australia on a visit, and two years later returned and settled here.

In 1982 Alex and Marika Weinberger joined the Australian Association of Jewish Holocaust Survivors, and Marika went on to become a board member. Three years later she attended an international gathering for Holocaust survivors in Sydney. In 1991 John Saunders, a fellow survivor, invited Marika onto the planning committee for the new Sydney Jewish Museum; Alex helped set up the museum library. That year Marika also became the president of the Australian Association of Jewish Holocaust Survivors and Descendants, a position she held for nine years. She is now Vice-President of the Jewish Museum.

In the meantime, their daughters Catherine and Yvonne had married and left home. Only then did

Marika Cierer Weinberger

Marika Weinberger in 1992. Photo courtesy Sydney Jewish Museum.

Marika and Alex break their long silence and begin to talk about their experiences during the war. Alex Weinberger died in July 1994, followed five months later by Edita.

How did Marika Weinberger survive the Holocaust when six million Jews perished? 'I've asked myself why I survived. Why me? I can claim very little credit. I can't say I survived because I did such and such. I believe in fate. And I had a lot of support.' That survival left her with a strong sense of responsibility — to the past and to the future. 'To prove I had the right to survive, I had to do something. Only if I work for the Holocaust survivors and their interest and aims is my survival worthwhile for me. It means I've done something with my life.'

Until now Marika and her generation, which she calls the Anne Frank generation, have run the Museum and acted as guides, telling the story of the Holocaust to visitors. When she gave up the presidency of the Association, Marika asked for a training program for guides to be set up at the Museum. Her daughter Yvonne is in the program. 'I'm beginning to see a future,' says Marika. 'I don't have to worry about what's going to happen when we're gone. I know the history of the Holocaust will be preserved.'

Marika Cierer Weinberger

The War Against the Jews

In 1933 Adolf Hitler and his Nazi Party came to power in Germany. Hitler's goal was to dominate Europe and establish a German empire — the Third Reich. He was also a rabid anti-Semite, determined to rid Europe of its Jewish population. The Nazis immediately began to exclude Jews from the professions, and built the first concentration camp, Dachau, to imprison their political opponents. In 1936 Germany signed military alliances with Italy and Japan.

As the first step in his expansion program — what the Germans called *Lebensraum*, or 'room to live' — Hitler annexed Austria in March 1938. Czechoslovakia was next. Unwilling to go to war over Czechoslovakia, Britain and France stood by while Germany occupied the Sudetenland, which had a large German population. This was legitimised in the Munich Agreement, in which Britain and France accepted the annexation of the Sudetenland. That same year, the Nuremberg Laws were passed, stripping Jews of their civil rights.

In November 1938, Herschel Grynszpan, a Jew, assassinated a German diplomat in Paris. Anti-Semitic riots broke out in Germany and Austria. On what came to be called *Kristallnacht*, because of the amount of broken glass in the streets, synagogues were burnt down and shops were looted. Soon after, 26 000 Jews were arrested and sent to concentration camps, and Jewish children were excluded from German schools. By 1939 the Nazis had built concentration camps for men at Buchenwald, Sachsenhausen, Flossenburg and Mauthausen, and one at Ravensbrück for women. As well as Jews, the Nazis sent Communists, homosexuals, criminals and Gypsies — whom they considered to be 'anti-social elements' — to the camps. Since the early 1930s they had also been exterminating people with physical and intellectual disabilities in hospitals and institutions.

On 15 March 1939, the Germans occupied the Czechoslovakian provinces of Bohemia-Moravia and Slovakia (where Marika Cierer and her family lived). Hungary took control of the third province, Ruthenia, which included Kosice (where the Cierers' extended family lived).

In August 1939 the Nazis signed a non-aggression pact with Russia, meaning that Russia would not interfere with their expansion east. The following month the German army invaded Poland. Realising belatedly that appeasement — giving in to Hitler — was not working, France and Britain declared war on Germany on 3 September 1939. Meanwhile, the Soviet Union occupied eastern Poland. In October, the first Jews were deported from Austria and

Moravia to concentration camps in Nazi-occupied Poland.

In April 1940 Germany invaded Denmark and Norway, and in May moved into Holland, Belgium and France. Driven back to Dunkirk, the British forces were evacuated from France. On 22 June France surrendered to Germany. In September the German–Italian–Japanese alliance — the Axis — was formed.

In June 1941 the German Army attacked its former ally, the Soviet Union. The following month, Reinhardt Heydrich, the German Gauleiter or commander in Czechoslovakia, was appointed by the Nazi High Command to oversee 'the final solution', Hitler's code for the extermination of the Jews of Europe. In September, all Jews in the German Reich were ordered to wear a yellow star on their clothing which identified them as Jewish, and the following month, they began to be deported. Jews were being massacred all over the Reich.

On 7 December 1941 Japan attacked the American Navy fleet at Pearl Harbour; the following day the United States entered the war on the side of Britain and France, forming the Allied forces.

On 20 January 1942 a conference of the German High Command was held in Wannsee to plan 'the final solution'. By this time, a million Jews had already been murdered. Emigration of Jews was halted, and Europe was to be combed for Jews, who were to be rounded up and 'resettled' — that is, exterminated — in the east. Not all Jews went quietly to their deaths. In the Vilna Ghetto in Poland they began to fight back, and other resistance groups sprang up throughout Eastern Europe. Jews also joined groups of partisans fighting the Germans in the countryside. On 18 January 1943 the Jews in the Warsaw Ghetto rose up in revolt against the Germans. After weeks of fighting, the German Army moved in and liquidated the ghetto. Heinrich Himmler, head of the feared Gestapo and the SS, then ordered the liquidation of all Polish ghettoes. In September the Vilna Ghetto was destroyed.

When did the Allies find out that the Germans were systematically exterminating Europe's Jews? Reports about deportations and death camps began trickling out of Europe early in 1942. In mid-1943 the British and US governments held a special meeting in Bermuda to discuss the 'Jewish problem'. By then they knew that the Jews of France, Belgium, Holland and Norway had been all but wiped out. However, they decided that rather than divert air or ground forces from the war effort to save Jews, they would concentrate on trying to win the war quickly, thus ending the threat to the Jews.

Between 15 May and 8 June 1944, with brutal efficiency, the Germans deported 476 000

Hungarians to Auschwitz Concentration Camp in the infamous Hungarian *Aktion*. Though Germany had clearly lost the war against the Allies, it continued to wage war against the Jews. By then the Allies knew about Auschwitz. Britain's Foreign Secretary, Anthony Eden, tried to persuade the Air Force to bomb the camp in July, but the Secretary of State for Air refused, arguing that Auschwitz was too far away for Allied bombers and too great a diversion of British forces. Soon after, however, a squadron of US aircraft passed close to Auschwitz on their way to drop supplies to the starving citizens of Warsaw. Allied planes also bombed factories — such as a synthetic oil and rubber plant where 30 000 slave labourers worked — near the concentration camp.

Auschwitz Concentration Camp.

Throughout the rest of the war Allied bombers continued to fly over Auschwitz, but never bombed it.

Meanwhile, on 6 June 1944, the Allies landed at Normandy, invading Nazi-occupied Western Europe. On 23 June, Russia — which had started out as Germany's ally but had changed sides after the German Army invaded their country in 1941 — began their offensive. The following day, they liberated the first concentration camp, Majdanek, outside Lublin in Poland. By 23 October the Allies had fought their way to France and liberated Paris. Realising the end was in sight, the Nazis began trying to hide evidence of the death camps. In November, Himmler ordered Rudolf Höss, the commandant of Auschwitz, to destroy the gas chambers and the crematoria, the great ovens which were used to burn the bodies of camp inmates.

Too late for its Jews, the Russians reached Warsaw on 17 January 1945. On 27 January the Soviet Army captured Auschwitz. In March the Americans reached the Rhine River in the heart of Germany. In April the Americans liberated Buchenwald concentration camp and the British liberated Bergen-Belsen. When the Russians and American troops met at the Elba River on 25 April, the Allies had won the war. Adolf Hitler committed suicide in a bunker beneath Berlin on 30 April, and on 7 May Germany surrendered unconditionally, ending the war in

Europe. When Japan surrendered in August, World War II was over.

On 22 November 1945, the Nuremberg War Crimes Tribunal, consisting of judges from England, North America and the Soviet Union, began trying top Nazis for war crimes. Of twenty-two defendants in the first round of trials, twelve — including Rudolf Höss, the commandant of Auschwitz, and Heinrich Himmler, architect of the death camps — were sentenced to death, three to life imprisonment and four to various prison terms. Three were acquitted, and Air Marshall Hermann Goering committed suicide in jail. Heydrich had been murdered in Czechoslovakia in May 1941 by two Czech agents flown in from England. Many leading Nazis escaped capture, however. In 1962, agents from Mossad, the Israeli Intelligence organisation, abducted Adolf Eichmann — one of the prime organisers of the final solution — from South America and, after a trial in Israel, he was executed. Josef Mengele, the Angel of Death, escaped to Brazil in South America after the war and died of natural causes in 1979.

Meanwhile, Jews liberated from concentration camps went home to try to re-establish their lives and find their relatives. They had no papers and no money, and when they reached their home towns, many found they no longer had a home. Often neighbours had moved into their property. Displaced persons camps were set up to process these homeless Jews and to try to reunite them with family members. Unable to settle back into their old home countries, many emigrated — to the United States, South Africa, New Zealand, Australia, Sweden. Others went to Palestine. The League of Nations (forerunner to the United Nations) had given Britain a mandate in 1922 to govern Palestine and establish a Jewish homeland there. But the British were afraid that a sudden influx of Jews would upset the delicate balance between Jews and Arabs in Palestine, and started turning refugee ships away. Many Jews entered the country illegally and a war broke out between Jewish guerilla fighters (determined to reclaim their homeland) and the British Army. The British moved out in 1948 and Palestine became the state of Israel.

Between four and six million Jews were murdered by the Nazis between 1933 and 1945.

Brigitte Muir

The View from the Top of the World

Brigitte Muir on top of Shishapangma's West Summit, 1994.
Photo courtesy Brigitte Muir.

In 1988 Brigitte Muir embarked on a quest to climb the Seven Summits, the highest peak on each continent. Nine years later, she achieved her dream, becoming the first Australian woman to climb Mount Everest, the world's highest mountain, and the only Australian to conquer the Seven Summits.

Brigitte Koch was born on 8 September 1958 and brought up in the Belgian steel-working town of Jemeppe in the industrial Meuse Valley. The closest thing to mountains in Jemeppe were the slag heaps from the old mining days that Brigitte used to climb with her sister and cousins.

When she was 16, Brigitte visited a fair with her friend Carine and saw an advertisement for a caving club. She and Carine joined up. 'I was curious,' she says. 'I didn't find the idea scary at all. It was something new to discover.' In the end, Carine wasn't allowed to go, but Brigitte went despite her mother's strenuous objections. After brief lessons in abseiling and using ladders, Brigitte was told to be ready on Saturday at 6.00 a.m.

Her first cave was Le Trou Wynant, in the middle of a forest. About 26 metres deep, it could have been bottomless as far as Brigitte was concerned. Excited and scared, she followed the leaders up a narrow, slippery trail into the cave's entrance, a rock window opening into darkness. Spooky voices echoed out of a 40-metre well just past the entrance. Queued up with ten other cavers for the rope, Brigitte wondered what she'd let herself in for. 'My turn came. I swallowed hard and the cave engulfed me. With eyes bulging in the semi-darkness, I managed to tie on my abseiling device, and started the descent on wobbly legs. I could see pinpoints of light at the bottom, and hear voices reverberating on the walls of the well. Whoo-ee, this was fun!'

Caving became an obsession, and Brigitte eventually became co-leader of the group. They would practise abseiling and jumaring — climbing up ropes with clamps — in an ancient mine shaft in the citadel of Liege. In time, Brigitte had explored all the caves within 30 kilometres of her home.

The summer she turned 17, Brigitte went on a climbing trip to the Jura Mountains in France. She quickly discovered that climbing was a lot more physically demanding than caving. 'Mountaineering is dangerous,' she says. 'You have to have the right education and training. I got my knowledge from climbing with friends who knew how to do it, by doing it with people more experienced than I was. Later I was ready to do it without people stronger than I was.

'People want to jump in the deep end, but you have to start simple and get the basics right rather than relying on other people and putting your life in their hands. As you do more climbing, you get a gut feeling about the right and wrong things to do.'

Climbing is mentally demanding, too. 'You have to be curious, to want to know how far you can push yourself into the unknown,' she says. 'You have to use your skills to deal with problems. Climbing is about problem solving. And of course it requires common sense and mental strength. It's not glamorous. You're always too hot or too cold and you have to carry a heavy pack, but the rewards are amazing.'

Brigitte's first real mountain climb was Gran Paradiso in Italy; it was 4000 metres high. 'It was a nice climb, very exciting,' she recalls. Before long, it would look very tame.

In 1979 Brigitte met Camille Piraprez, who had climbed in Canada. She talked him into joining her on a climb up the Lotus Flower Tower in the Yukon's Logan Mountains. Now studying archaeology at university, Brigitte got a job in a supermarket to pay for the adventure.

The pair flew to the Yukon, and pitched their tents in a field in Tungsten. Later they learned it was the town tip and the favourite haunt of grizzly bears. It wasn't till they'd flown in by helicopter to the Cirque of the Unclimbables, a horseshoe area enclosed by

Brigitte Muir

Brigitte and Camille Piraprez in the Cirque of the Unclimbables, 1979.
Photo courtesy Brigitte Muir.

incredibly sharp, steep granite towers, that Brigitte realised this was real, not a fantasy any more.

Brigitte and Camille were alone in the wilderness for twenty days. After several attempts, they made it to the Upper Meadow at 4000 metres and started climbing, but when it began to snow they decided to abseil back down. As well as learning something about climbing on that expedition, Brigitte learned something about herself: 'I needed to go somewhere else, soon, and I would always need to have somewhere to go, somebody to meet. A mountain to climb.'

After that taste of freedom in Canada, Brigitte could not settle down to life as an archaeologist in Belgium. She considered going to Kenya, but let a travel agent talk her into visiting Australia. She knew nothing about this country except that it was big, far away and had kangaroos. It was on the obligatory grand tour of Australia by campervan with three friends that she discovered Mount Arapiles, a row of crumbling, orange cliffs outside the town of Horsham in north-western Victoria. At the camp site there she met and fell for Roddy Mackenzie, who accompanied the tourists to the Blue Mountains near Sydney. On the way they stopped off in Wollongong to pick up his friend, the climber Jon Muir. Roddy and Jon invited Brigitte on a world climbing tour they were planning for 1982, starting with Changabang in northern India.

Torn between her life in Belgium and Roddy in Australia, Brigitte travelled backwards and forwards for a time, but the death of a friend in a climbing accident made the decision for her — she would leave Europe. Traumatised, she flew to India and joined the Changabang expedition.

As the relationship between Brigitte and Roddy cooled, a spark ignited between Brigitte and Jon. A few months later Jon met Brigitte's parents in Belgium, and they were married in Jemeppe in 1983. Jon's parents bought them a tent as a wedding present, and they settled at the foot of the Arapiles. The area was a climber's paradise, and Brigitte and Jon hired themselves out as guides.

In 1984 Jon was invited on a six-man expedition to climb the West Ridge of Mount Everest without supplementary oxygen or the help of Sherpas, the expert Nepalese mountain guides. In those days, Jon was the serious climber in the family. He was much stronger and more experienced than Brigitte, and she stood in awe of him. But she also worried about him. While Jon was on the mountain, Brigitte went to the Everest Base Camp to go trekking with her younger sister, Veronique.

It turned into a long expedition, two months of hardship and constant fear. Brigitte's fears were justified. Returning to Base Camp after a climb with Veronique one day, she learned that two climbers had been killed. Realising the conditions were not good enough for a summit attempt, Jon's group had decided to turn back. Soon afterwards, Craig Nottle, one of the climbers, was taken by an avalanche. Fred From and Kim Logan, who were a couple of hundred metres ahead, noticed that something was wrong below and also started back. Fred lost his footing and fell all the way to the bottom of Everest's North Face into Tibet. Jon returned safely. 'I was very scared on Everest in 1984,' recalls Brigitte. 'I had a gut feeling that Jon might die. After that, I decided it would be better to climb with Jon than to wait at the bottom.'

On this expedition she also met American millionaire Dick Bass, who'd recently finished climbing the highest mountain on each continent — the Seven Summits. This put an idea into Brigitte's head — she would climb the Seven Summits. 'Some people who want to do the climb are trophy hunting, but what I wanted was a long-term goal,' she says. 'I was good at starting things, but not so good at finishing them. I wanted a project I'd start and finish.'

Meanwhile, Brigitte and Jon's marriage was in trouble. On a 1986 climb up Mount Shivling in the Himalayas they fought bitterly. When they returned to Australia, Brigitte moved into a house with friends in Melbourne and got a job. Part of the problem was that the Muirs were in the same field, but Jon was a much stronger climber than Brigitte. 'After a while you feel overshadowed,' she says. 'When I came to Australia, I lived through him. I was the hero's wife. Suddenly it wasn't enough any more.'

In 1987 some friends asked Brigitte to join an expedition to the 8000-metre Hidden Peak in the Karakorum in Pakistan in July and August. Planning an expedition to Mount Everest in September with Peter Hillary — whose father Edmund Hillary had been, with Tenzing Norgay, one of the first two people to reach the summit of Mount Everest — Jon talked Brigitte into accompanying him to the Gangotri in India for training. Broke, Brigitte had to beg a couple of thousand dollars from a sponsor and the airfare from her father to fly to Pakistan.

Brigitte's goal was to regain her confidence as a climber, not to reach the summit. 'I was too busy learning self-sufficiency and contentment, and conquering a fragile self-esteem to worry about such trifling matters,' she says. The expedition turned into a nightmare for everybody and had to be called off. India and Pakistan were at war, and Indian soldiers were shelling Pakistani climbers on a peak on the border. None of the group's climbers 'summited', and four Pakistanis climbing alongside Brigitte were killed in an avalanche.

Determined to salvage something, a group decided to climb Gasherbrum Two, another 8000-metre peak in the Everest group. Brigitte joined them. But after Camp One, it became clear that her body could not handle the altitude. At 6000 metres, the air contains only one-third to a half of the oxygen it carries at sea level. To operate at high altitudes, the body has to make more red blood cells to distribute more oxygen to the muscles and nerves. It takes about three to five weeks to adjust to high altitudes. Newcomers to high altitudes can experience headaches, dizziness, nausea and palpitations. The best way to acclimatise is to climb to a new altitude carrying your gear, come down and sleep at a lower altitude, then move up again. Having already spent ten days above 6500 metres while trying to climb Hidden Peak, Brigitte had stayed too high for too long. Her body started to weaken. She had to descend, alone. That climb turned into a terrifying ordeal.

As she prepared to go down, Brigitte realised two things: the men had her lighter, and she had lost a contact lens. These are minor irritations on the ground: on a mountain they can be lethal. Without her contact lens, she had trouble keeping her balance on the steep ground. Without a lighter to melt snow to drink, she could die of dehydration — a climber needs six to eight litres of fluid a day. To survive, she would have to go all the way down to Base Camp. That meant negotiating a treacherous icefall on her own. Frighteningly unstable, this collapsed glacier was littered with steep crevasses and ice cliffs. Since she wasn't roped to a partner, any fall — from a collapsed ice bridge, or into a crevasse — would be fatal.

Brigitte had no choice; she had to get down. At the icefall, she faced her first crevasses — two bottomless holes more than a metre wide. What should she do? Should she take off her pack, throw it across the gap and jump after it? No — when she tried it, her pack was too heavy to throw. Could she jump across? It was that or die here. Sitting on the ground with her back to the pack, she strapped it on, swivelled around on her knees and stood up. Then she ran like mad and jumped. She made it. It was only the first of many crevasses.

This was the most frightening experience of Brigitte Muir's climbing career. 'I spent all day jumping crevasses in terrible danger,' she recalls. 'But after the first crevasse, I kept a cool head and dealt with it. I didn't panic. There are situations where you can't afford to panic. You have to look at your skills and talk yourself into taking certain risks ... I had no choice but to get down.'

It took her all day. The last obstacle was an 80-centimetre wide torrent raging between steep icy shores within sight of Base Camp. Tired as Brigitte was by now, it seemed impossible ... Then someone from Base Camp saw her and threw her a rope, which was then used to drag her across the chasm. She was weak with relief.

Undaunted by her close call, Brigitte set about organising the first climb in her Seven Summits' quest — Mount McKinley, the highest mountain in North America. Called Denali by the locals, the Alaskan mountain is 6194 metres high. As her climbing partner, she chose Al Sweetman, her old housemate from Melbourne. To fund the trip, she picked grapes and raised some sponsorship money. May 1988 found Brigitte and Al in Alaska. From Talkeetna, they flew to Kahiltna International Airport, a tent village on the eastern branch of the Kahiltna Glacier. This was no luxury expedition; the toilet, a wooden throne, was visible to anyone coming back from the mountain. Brigitte hid behind an umbrella.

Al on skis, Brigitte on foot, they set off to the summit pulling heavy sleds. It was blustery and cold so close to the Arctic Circle, but also light 24 hours

Australian Heroines

a day, meaning they could climb whenever they wanted. At the notorious Windy Corner, Brigitte got frostbite on her stomach when the metal karabiner holding her harness touched her skin. At 5150 metres the weather was so bad they had to spend three nights waiting, which gave Brigitte time to acclimatise. Next day they set off and made it to the top, meeting three Korean climbers there. Brigitte had climbed the first of her seven summits. They made a grand entrance to Base Camp, with Al on skis towing Brigitte on a sled. Later, Brigitte heard that Jon had climbed Mount Everest on 28 May, four days after she'd reached the summit of Denali.

Having fallen in love with Alaska, Brigitte decided to stay on, and found a job as a bartender at the Fairview Inn, a wild pub in Talkeetna. But she still intended to pursue her goal. In February 1989, she flew to Tanzania to climb the 5895-metre Mount Kilimanjaro, Africa's highest peak. She hired porters to accompany her on the climb up the rarely trodden Umbwe Route. Kilimanjaro was exotic, dense forest with white monkeys in the tree canopy becoming short alpine grass at 4200 metres, and volcanic ash higher up. At the top, hand in hand in a howling wind, Brigitte and her guide walked towards Uhuru Peak. She had notched up her second summit.

With two summits under her belt, Brigitte had to make a decision — give up the Seven Summits and return to Alaska, or continue on her quest? She chose mountaineering and, after a sojourn in Belgium, returned to Australia — and Jon. Having climbed Mount Everest, Jon was turning his attention to the Australian wilderness. 'Maybe that's why we got back together,' says Brigitte. 'There was not so much competition any more. I had started my own project and felt better about it all.'

Brigitte got a job and started saving for her next trip — Aconcagua in Argentina. This time she would go solo. In Argentina, mules carried her gear to Base Camp, and after crossing the Horcones River, knees trembling with cold and adrenalin, she spent twelve hours walking the 42 kilometres to Plaza de Mulas at 4200 metres. After a night at Campo Berlin, the last camp before the summit, Brigitte set off on the last leg, worrying about what would happen if she got lost, alone on the mountain. She quickly hit her stride, overtaking everyone on the trail except a Japanese climber. The last scree, the Canaletta, was a nightmare, vertical and unstable and covered with loose boulders and stones. But finally, after a last push, she was on the summit. It was Christmas Day. She shook hands with the Japanese climber and took photos. When he left, Brigitte found herself alone on the highest mountain in South America. 'I walked a few steps around the large sloping expanse, looked towards the Pacific Ocean and burst into tears.'

Brigitte's fourth summit was a much less arduous experience than the first three. In May 1990, she, Jon and some friends climbed Mount Kosciuszko, which, at 2228 metres, is Australia's highest mountain. For Brigitte, this climb was a sheer delight — friends, fine weather and fun. And after years of feeling foreign in Australia, she finally felt that she was in her own landscape. After passing a string of crystalline lakes, they reached the summit on 28 May. Exhilarated, they ran from boulder to boulder gazing at the innumerable peaks below. This time there were no worries about getting down safely. They pitched their tents on the summit and watched the sunset. The only hardship occurred when a fox slunk into the camp during the night and stole their chocolate!

Later the same year, Brigitte, Jon and a film crew flew to Russia to climb Mount Elbrus, the highest peak in Europe. Mount Elbrus had a reputation: six months before, twenty climbers had lost their way on the mountain and died. In Leningrad — now St Petersburg — Brigitte was feted as 'the famous Australian mountaineer'. Along with competitors in a climbing race, the Australians made it to the top. It was Brigitte's fifth summit: two to go. Those last two summits would turn out to be the hardest.

It would be three years before Brigitte could undertake her sixth summit. With Australia experiencing an economic recession, money was tight. To stay afloat, the Muirs started Adventure Plus, their own mountaineering business, based in Natimuk in Victoria. Then, in 1993, they were offered places on a big commercial expedition to the North Face of Mount Everest. Jon would climb for free in return for acting as a guide, and Brigitte would only have to pay cost price. As places on these expeditions usually cost between US$30 000 and US$65 000, it was an irresistible chance for Brigitte to have a go at Everest.

The team acclimatised in Nepal, then crossed into Tibet early in September. It was then that Brigitte caught her first terrifying and tantalising glimpse of Mount Everest — Chomolungma, the Goddess Mother of Earth. Nervously listening to a lecture on oxygen at the Base Camp, she wondered if she could do this climb, which would be her first attempt at climbing higher than 8000 metres.

It went wrong from the start. Brigitte wasn't fit enough, and she'd been smoking to calm her nerves. The climb to Interim Camp at 5800 metres was a breathless torture. Her confidence plummeted. Somehow she huffed and puffed her way up to the North Col Camp. But when Jon and the stronger climbers set off to establish Camp Two at 7400 metres, she stayed behind. 'This mountain was so big! Its North Face, which was right in front of us, soaring 3000 metres to the summit, was totally overwhelming and drained my energy. I felt insignificant.'

When Brigitte suffered stomach trouble, and Jon came down with bronchitis, the Muirs decided to return to Base Camp. By now, Brigitte was jittery and trembling, and felt out of control. Despite this, she joined a group going up to Advanced Base Camp to help two climbers summit. Wind turned the two hopefuls back and heavy snowfalls destroyed Camp Two. The next morning the team returned to Advanced Base Camp to rest and wait for milder weather. One of the men became ill and had to be piggybacked down to Base Camp, where he died. He was buried near the old British Camp Two.

While several people summited, Jon and Brigitte squeezed into a tent with another climber at 7600 metres. When clouds came in, they packed and started down towards the North Col. Losing her balance, Brigitte sat down in the snow and burst into tears. Jon's anger bucked her up enough to get down, but she felt guilty and ashamed: she knew Jon had missed out on summiting because he'd stayed with her. While helping to pack the tents and gear, Brigitte had a bad turn and had to be put on oxygen. It was the high-altitude climber's nemesis: cerebral oedema, a swelling of the brain caused by lack of oxygen, leading to headaches, disorientation, a racing heart and vomiting. Once again, two weeks at 6400 metres had been too much for her body.

Having failed to reach the top of Mount Everest,

Brigitte climbed Shishapangma in the Himalayas in May 1994 with a team from Out There Trekking. Safely back in Base Camp she let go and cried: she'd finally reached the magic number — 8000 metres.

At the beginning of the Seven Summits project, Brigitte had been funding her climbs herself, but now she needed sponsors to finance more expensive climbs. 'I wasn't very good at marketing myself,' she admits. 'I spent a year trying to raise money and only got a thousand dollars — I would have been better off getting a job and saving for the money. Fortunately, I had friends who were happy to blow my trumpet for me.' They found sponsors for her sixth summit, Mount Vinson in Antarctica, as well as her next Everest attempt.

In November 1994, Brigitte and John Coll, who was paying her to be his guide, flew to Punta Arenas in Patagonia in South America, where they picked up another team member, Ross Nichols. It was eighteen days before the weather cleared sufficiently to fly into Patriot Hills. In Antarctica at last, Brigitte was overwhelmed by the eerie strangeness and beauty of this last wilderness.

At Patriot Hills Brigitte added another guide, Aaron, to her team. When the fog lifted, they flew into a valley of snow at the foot of a huge rock wall. Six hours of pulling sleds got them to Camp One the next day. After a fitful night's sleep battling the relentless light, they climbed to Camp Two, where they had to leave the sleds. At the top of the icefall they encountered a maze of deep crevasses covered with a thin layer of ice and snow. Miraculously, these held under their weight.

After waiting out a day of bad weather, they plodded up a steep rise to the plateau leading to Vinson summit. Buffeted by a vicious wind, they donned their warmest gear, insulated with goose down. Brigitte started up a slope leading to summit ridge, but by this time John was flagging. They reached camp in a total white-out, a dangerous snow condition where it's impossible to distinguish the ground from the horizon. They awoke on Christmas Day to an Arctic gale, their sleeping bags drenched by showers of frozen condensation from the inside of the tent and the ground wet under their sleeping mats. They dug themselves out and celebrated Christmas Day with a packet of sliced ham Brigitte had saved for the occasion.

When the weather cleared they descended to Base Camp to rest. Time was of the essence now. If they were going to get back to Patriot Hills in time to catch the plane out, they would have to attempt the summit the next day, then race back down. Driven back by the wind a couple of times, Brigitte, Ross and Aaron set off again at 5.00 p.m. John had left Base Camp and was on his way home. It was so appallingly cold Brigitte was wearing a neoprene face mask with a cold air mask over it, a polartec suit, a windsuit and a downsuit. Puffing madly, they made a dash for the summit ridge. Unroped, they started climbing towards the summit — and made it. It was just midnight. Shivering uncontrollably, they took photographs. 'It's the coldest place I've ever been,' says Brigitte. But it was also the most beautiful.

Roping up again, they powered back down. The last hour of the descent was terrifying, with huge areas of freshly dumped snow settling under their feet with thundering crashes. Somehow they made it to Base Camp in time to catch the plane.

Brigitte now had only one summit to climb — which meant facing Everest again. In April 1995 Brigitte and Jon joined an Out There Trekking expedition to the North Ridge of Mount Everest for her second attempt from the Tibetan side of the Himalayas. She was not scared this time, nor as overawed by her husband. 'I had earned my high-altitude ribbons on Shishapangma without him, and for once realised that although I would never be as strong as Jon, I could certainly be stronger than a lot of people.' It was a big expedition, with eighteen westerners, twelve Sherpas and three company guides. It was Jon's fifth Everest climb — again he had come along only to help Brigitte fulfil her dream.

Although several members of this expedition

made it to the summit, Brigitte baulked at Camp Three at 8200 metres. Her heart wasn't in it. 'It was a puzzling feeling, but I could only surrender to it. And thank God I did.' The next day she found out why: Jon was ill and needed to go down, fast. He was having trouble breathing, and had to go on oxygen. When they staggered into Advanced Base Camp, a doctor diagnosed bronchitis and conjunctivitis.

Having come so far, Brigitte refused to give up. She joined the last group to attempt the summit. The climb had an inauspicious beginning. First, she found herself last on the line at the ropes which started above Camp Three. Then when the others moved off, Brigitte noticed that her head torch was growing dim. She called out to the others to wait, but they did not hear her. Not concerned yet, she tried to fix the torch, but the spare batteries did not work. Meanwhile, the wind had picked up, and the line she was clipped to had disappeared into the darkness. The three men in the team had vanished, leaving her behind. She was alone in the dark on the North Face of Everest.

'At the time I was very angry,' recalls Brigitte. 'The others did not do what they were supposed to do — you're always supposed to look after your climbing partners. But then they were not as acclimatised as I was, and their brains were not working as well as mine … And the man in front of me was young and scared. When I called out for them to wait, they didn't hear me. Mind you, those in front should have known to keep an eye on the rest of us … But I was angry, not scared. I knew I could look after myself on the mountain.'

Brigitte did not trust the ropes enough to go up, but could not see well enough to go down. She made her way back to a tiny rock shelf and sat down with her back to the wind. Her pack, holding two bottles of oxygen, was her only protection from the icy wind. There she waited, searching for any sign of sunrise, afraid to fall asleep in case she died of hypothermia. At dawn, driven by anger and determination, she stumbled down to Camp Three, where she huddled in her sleeping bag, sobbing and shivering uncontrollably for hours. To make matters worse, she wasn't able to have another try at the summit because there were no Sherpas available to help her if anything went wrong.

For a long time afterwards, Brigitte would lie awake at night replaying the events of that terrible climb. 'I've been to lots of 8000-metre peaks and didn't summit. It's all part of the growing process. But in this instance, I knew I could have gone to the summit because I was so strong. I was very disappointed. I grieved about it for months.'

Brigitte decided she couldn't give up on climbing Everest, even though she'd promised Jon she wouldn't try again. 'I was trapped. I had to finish what I'd started and re-conquer my self-confidence, or die of shame and self-pity. I had to go back.' But she would not put Jon through it again: next time she would go alone.

Her opportunity came in April 1996, when she joined a no-frills expedition to the South Side of Everest, entering from Nepal. At the Base Camp she met up with Rob Hall, whose Adventure Consultants expedition had been too expensive for her, and old friends from Scott Fisher's big commercial expedition.

The first challenge was the dangerous Khumbu icefall. Holding onto a safety rope, Brigitte followed the others in crampons — spiked boots — across aluminium ladders tied together by string, balanced across bottomless chasms — all the time carrying a 17-kilogram pack containing her tent, a stove, extra food, a still camera, a video camera and a tape recorder. On this climb, she would have to cross the terrifying icefall eight times: four times up and four times down. By the time she reached Camp Two her hips were sore and she had diarrhoea.

As avalanches were occurring more regularly, the season was fast becoming a disaster, but Brigitte decided to press on. As she jumared up the vertical pitch, she passed Sherpas helping down a Taiwanese man who'd slid head first into a crevasse. When she reached Camp Three, the commercial groups were moving slowly towards Camp Four. Next morning, Brigitte set off at 11.00 a.m. The weather was worsening, with high winds, snow in flurries and low visibility. Ahead, a huge snow plume covered the upper reaches of the mountain, but the climbers continued on. By the time Brigitte reached the tents on the South Col, she was shivering uncontrollably and her hands no longer worked. She put on her down suit and moaned as the circulation returned painfully to her hands.

Waking at 2.00 a.m., Brigitte shivered till morning, when she heard the bad news. Five people had fallen from the South Summit. Despite this, Brigitte's group decided to hang around for another day and give the summit a shot. That night the wind was so strong Brigitte had to hang onto her tent to stop it being blown away. By then, Rob Hall and Scott Fisher had died.

Brigitte's group had to go down. On the way she helped a climber who'd spent two nights out in the storm; his face was black and his arm frozen to the elbow. After a memorial service for the dead, it was crunch time. Brigitte and a partner decided to go up again, but the Sherpas refused to go higher than Camp Four. In the end they ran out of time and had to descend without summiting. But Brigitte was content. She'd done her best, and she'd survived.

Back in Australia, Jon wanted her to wait before

making another attempt, but Brigitte knew she had to return as soon as possible. Everest wasn't just the highest mountain in the world, it was the Seventh Summit. And as she had decided to make only one more attempt, this would be her last chance to climb it.

In April 1997 Brigitte joined an expedition to Mount Everest and Mount Lhotse led by Mal Duff. On her Everest team were Mal and three young Mexican climbers. This time Brigitte was filming the ascent for a television network. Determined to give herself the best possible chance, she hired a Sherpa to carry her gear up. All went well till 21 April, at Camp Two, when Brigitte awoke at 6400 metres with a sore throat, throbbing sinuses and a cough. It took forever to get ready to leave the tent. First she had to boil up two litres of fluid, then she defrosted her contact lenses on the heat of her stomach. She drank three coffees, took her vitamin tablets, picked up the pack she'd prepared the night before, and had breakfast. Finally, she drank another two cups of tea to keep up her liquid intake. Descending to Base Camp, she ran into Mal and thought he looked ill. That night he died in his tent, not quite 44. A helicopter took his body away, and the climbers held a wake.

After a rest and some antibiotics for her sinuses, Brigitte went up again, reaching Camp Three. Several teams were gearing up for a rush to the summit, but as she wanted to wait for the right weather to go up again, she went back to Base Camp for a rest before her summit attempt. When the weather was still not improving up high, she went down to Dingoche to allow her body to recuperate at a lower level. None of the others made it to the top — the weather was too bad. With only thirteen days till her permit to climb Mount Everest expired, Brigitte kept her nerve and sat tight.

On 21 May, she made her last trek through the icefall. Her group of six had now shrunk to four — herself and one of the Mexicans, and two Sherpas, Dorje and Kipa, who had decided to join Brigitte on her summit attempt. The Sherpas were raring to go, but Brigitte insisted on taking her time; she wasn't her strongest at these altitudes, and she'd been ill too often. By 23 May, despite a bad weather forecast, fifteen people had summited, including her Mexican friend. The following day, as weather forecasts predicted ideal conditions up high, Brigitte ascended to Camp Three. She was moving at her own pace, hoping to summit on 26 May. Exhausted, half-dead climbers straggled past her on their way down. Then Brigitte was left alone in the big tent. It was too cold and windy to go up that day. That night she cried herself to sleep.

The next day was clear, with no wind. Brigitte

climbed up to the South Col, where she took oxygen and had a rest. It started to snow … then stopped. Brigitte prepared frantically. She and the Sherpas started moving at a quarter to one in the morning. A traverse across a wind slab took them close to the ascending ramp leading to the Balcony, a small shoulder on the ridge that led to the summit. At the Balcony, Brigitte stopped for a snack and photos. It was now dawn. After changing her oxygen bottle, she climbed around a snow slope to a section of snow and rock. The steps chopped by previous climbers had collapsed, and the going was hard in the crumbling snow. By now she had an irritating cough caused by cold air leaking into her oxygen mask.

Suddenly the ridge leading to the famous Hillary Step appeared. Kipa changed Brigitte's oxygen bottle, and they set off again. Desperate to descend in daylight, they went into overdrive. Brigitte began filming. Now she could see the summit. Excited, Kipa ran ahead to the top. Brigitte followed, not quite as fast. She shrugged out of her pack, took out her lucky koala Sheila, and made the last few steps. At 10.30 a.m. on 27 May 1997, Brigitte Muir became the first Australian woman to reach the summit of Mount Everest, and the first Australian to climb all Seven Summits. After making a tape for Australia and leaving a picture of herself and Jon, she put her gear back on and, without a backward glance, started back down again.

Brigitte Muir

On top of Everest, *27 May 1997.* Photo courtesy Brigitte Muir.

'There's no absolute bliss on the summit unless it's been easy, a low mountain where coming down is a piece of cake,' says Brigitte. 'Getting up is only half the job — coming down is more dangerous. Reaching the summit of Everest was a relief, relief that I didn't have to go any further or come back one more time. You let go a little bit but not too much. You have to stay focused because you have to concentrate on the way down. You can celebrate at the bottom. It takes a while to realise you've done it, especially if it's taken a long time.'

But there was to be no celebration at the bottom. With the media keen to get back to Australia,

Brigitte was whisked away by helicopter for a media conference in Kathmandu. 'I didn't have time to process it,' she says. 'I missed that amazing feeling at the end of an expedition when you realise you're safe and happy, and everybody has a big booze-up — the debriefing. I didn't have it after Everest. It was a real shame.'

The end of her nine-year project could have been a terrible anticlimax for Brigitte. Fortunately, writing a book about her life — *The Wind in My Hair* — kept her busy for a year. 'Writing the book was a real adventure, a lot of fun and pretty traumatic all in one,' she says. 'I realised what a soap opera my life was. I learned a lot about myself.

'I don't consider myself brave. Brave sounds like you don't know fear, but that's not the way it works. I'm realistic more than brave. You have to love what you're doing. Climbing is hard, painful and scary, but that's the fun. You're pushing yourself to your own limits.

'What I like is that everything feels very simple out there. There are no complications. You feel as if you understand the world.'

But when the book was finished, her old obsessions resurfaced, and she set out to climb another mountain. Then, within a short space of time, she lost two close friends in climbing accidents and had a change of heart. 'I've given up big peaks for the time being,' she says. 'There's too much sadness up there now. But I haven't given up adventures.'

And in 1998, after she'd climbed the Seven Summits and reached the top of Mount Everest, she began to understand why the Tibetans worshipped Mount Everest as the Goddess Mother of Earth. 'I was working as a guide in the Everest area, and I ended up in the valley that goes up to Everest,' she recalls. 'I looked up and saw the summit above me and fell to my knees. It's the only time I've ever had a religious experience. I had to kneel to the mountain.'

Samantha Miles

Surviving a Life-threatening Illness

Samantha Miles (at left) today, with her sister Katy and her mother, Cathy.
Photo courtesy Samantha Miles.

At 20, Samantha Miles was diagnosed with acute promyelocytic leukaemia and told she had three weeks to live. After six months of chemotherapy, she had a bone-marrow transplant and soon after was declared free of leukaemia. But Samantha discovered that surviving the illness was only the first stage of recovery. It took her another eight years to come to terms with the physical and emotional toll.

Samantha Miles was born in Sydney on 15 September 1971. From the age of 14 she lived in Dural, a semi-rural north-western suburb of Sydney, with her parents, Cathy and Ron, both teachers, and her sister Katy, who is fifteen months younger. Samantha was a shy and introverted child, who loved reading and riding horses. She completed her secondary school education at a local high school, which she found big, anonymous and intimidating.

After finishing the Higher School Certificate, Samantha enrolled in a Psychology degree at Macquarie University, but dropped out after a year. 'I did well, but I wasn't happy there,' she says. 'It was too impersonal. I was just another student in a class of 1500.' As she'd always been good at art, she transferred into a degree in design at the University of Newcastle. For Samantha, moving away from home was traumatic; she felt lonely and isolated in Newcastle. And for a girl used to having the run of acres of bush in Dural, the small industrial city was a shock — noisy, crowded and polluted. 'I lived in Adamstown in a fibro house on a main road next to a car yard,' says Samantha. 'All you could see when you looked out the window was rows of backyards and a horizon of brown smog.'

Some students easily combine studying with making friends and having fun; others find university a struggle. Samantha could not find the right balance in her life. A perfectionist, she worried constantly about her studies and had almost no social life. For four days a week she'd attend classes and study; on the weekends she'd drive back to Sydney to see her family, ride her horse and work part-time as a waiter in a Mexican restaurant. 'I never went to parties or had boyfriends,' she recalls.

At 19, she was close to a breakdown. 'I was pretty depressed around that time,' she says. She was haunted by the feeling that she wasn't making the most of her talents — that she wasn't fulfilling her potential. She was stalled. 'I'd think, "Someday I'm going to change this", but I hadn't found my role in life,' she says. 'And if I had, I wasn't sure I could do it.'

Samantha Miles

At the beginning of her second year at Newcastle, Samantha began to feel unwell. She tired easily, and wanted to lie down as soon as she came in from class. 'Even my bones felt tired,' she says. She bruised easily, but put this down to bumping herself while horse riding. Occasionally she would wake up in the middle of the night wanting to vomit, but the feeling would pass, and she'd ignore it. When she started having fainting fits, though, she sought medical help. Her family doctor could find nothing wrong with her. Another doctor thought she might be suffering from hypoglycaemia — or low blood-sugar levels — which can cause fainting. It wasn't till her urine turned a fluorescent orange colour that the alarm bells rang. Suspecting hepatitis, doctors at the university medical centre sent her blood and urine away for analysis.

The test results came back on 11 June 1992. After reading the results, a doctor dispatched a nurse to haul Samantha out of a classroom where she was doing an exam. Confused and anxious, Samantha followed her to the surgery, and sat stunned while a doctor told her she probably had leukaemia. The news was too overwhelming for her to take in. 'I just couldn't believe it,' she says. 'I asked the doctor if I was going to lose my hair, and she said, "Yes".'

Every minute counted; the doctors had made an appointment for Samantha with an oncologist — a cancer specialist — in Sydney that afternoon. 'Then they just pushed me out the door,' says Samantha. It was all too fast — one minute she'd been an ordinary university student doing an exam, the next she was a 'patient' with a life-threatening disease. Fortunately, Samantha's father was already on his way to Newcastle to take her home for the weekend; her fainting fits had made her afraid to drive. Ron Miles, then a deputy principal in a high school, was dazed by his daughter's news. He was so preoccupied on the way back that he could scarcely drive — they were two hours late for the appointment with the specialist.

The oncologist immediately did a painful bone-marrow biopsy. In this procedure, a large needle is pushed into the pelvic bones in the lower back and cells are removed for analysis. After a two-hour wait, the diagnosis was confirmed — Samantha did have leukaemia. Leukaemia is a malignant disease in which the bone marrow produces too many white cells, which then attack the immune system. It is often fatal, even when treated. The specialist outlined Samantha's treatment: three courses of chemotherapy followed by a bone-marrow transplant if the chemo worked. All going well, the bone-marrow transplant would take place in six months, around Christmas. Tests also showed that Samantha had inflamed kidneys and was bleeding internally, which accounted for the terrible nausea and the fluorescent orange urine.

Samantha Miles

The very next day she was admitted to a Sydney hospital to begin treatment. Her mother accompanied her, sleeping in a camp bed beside her. Samantha soon had her first taste of life as a cancer patient. It was a huge adjustment. A few days earlier she'd been running her own life; now she was helpless, dependent on what the doctors and nurses wanted to tell her. And she had to submit to being handled by strangers. For a shy, modest girl, the loss of privacy was hard to bear. She fought back as long as she could by dragging herself and the machines attached to her to the bathroom, rather than using a bedpan.

One of the initial tests showed that Samantha was severely anaemic. She was not allowed to shave her legs or brush her teeth, and was warned to avoid bumping herself in case she began to bleed. Because her white cells had begun attacking her immune system, she was placed on an intravenous drip containing blood platelets, a new drug called tretinoin acid (a highly-concentrated form of Vitamin A), and Maxolon for her inflamed liver. The doctors hoped that the tretinoin might reduce the rampage of leukaemic white cells and avert the need for more invasive chemotherapy.

To feed in the chemotherapy, blood transfusions and antibiotics, and to draw blood for testing, the doctors attempted to insert a Port-a-Cath — a small plastic disc connected to the veins around the heart

— into Samantha's chest. When two attempts failed, the doctors inserted a bigger device, a Hickman catheter, into the middle of her chest. Several muscles were cut during the operation, leaving Samantha with a violently aching shoulder — but at least she had a private room and her own toilet now. Because she was not allowed to wet the wound in her chest, the Hickman catheter made showering an ordeal, involving wrapping her chest in yards of cling wrap and fastening it with sticky tape. Sleep was impossible.

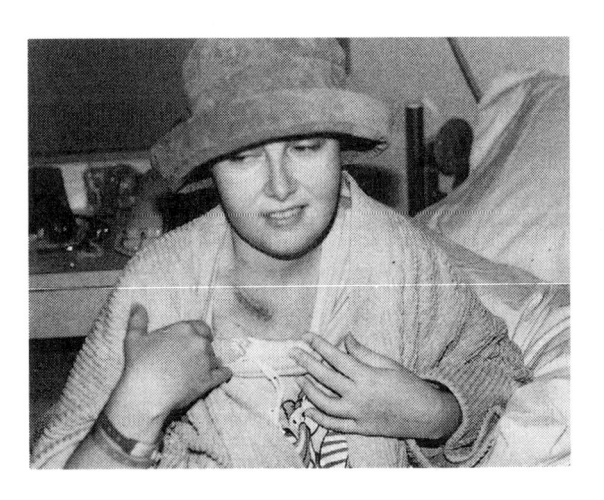

Samantha Miles shows her scars from the operation to insert her Hickman catheter. Photo courtesy Samantha Miles.

Unfortunately, the tretinoin did not work. Samantha had to start chemotherapy. Chemotherapy is toxic. At the time Samantha was having

Samantha Miles

her treatment, it not only destroyed the leukaemic cells, but it also destroyed all the body's other cells, such as platelets and red and white blood cells that are vital to the immune system. There are many side-effects, and these can be painful. Because it leaves the recipient so vulnerable to infection, even mouth ulcers, scratches, bruising or colds can have fatal consequences.

But after a week of chemotherapy, Samantha's leukaemia was still rampaging. Then, on 19 June, she began coughing. What began as an irritating, tickling cough quickly turned into a life-threatening problem. By 10.00 p.m. Samantha was fighting for breath. Concerned, she called for help. Then she began coughing up blood. An oxygen mask relieved the coughing for a while, but at three o'clock in the morning she suffered another violent coughing fit. She began to think she might be dying. 'I was drowning,' says Samantha. 'I was gurgling when I tried to speak because of the blood.' She had too much to think about to panic, she says. 'The most important thing was getting the next breath.' By 6.00 a.m. Samantha's hands and face were blue, and her eyes would not focus. The nurses called in Samantha's oncologist. At 9.00 a.m. Samantha's body collapsed. It was at this point that her mother, who'd been at her side all night, fell apart and was sent from the room.

Finally, covered in blood, Samantha was wheeled

into intensive care — and left alone. 'I was vaguely aware of what was going on,' she recalls. 'I was happy because I thought they were going to put me on a life-support machine.' But nothing happened. 'I realised that they didn't know what to do next,' she says. 'My vision was getting narrower and narrower, and I started to lose the feeling in my lower body. I realised then that I could die. That I was, in fact, dying.' Instead of giving up, Samantha was galvanised into fighting back. 'I was furious. I just kept saying to myself, "C'mon, get the next breath".'

Finally, a life-support machine arrived, and the doctors tried to pass a breathing tube down Samantha's throat. Despite the huge doses of morphine and sedatives Samantha had been given to calm her down, she fought against the tube. 'It felt huge,' she remembers. 'And they put another tube down beside the breathing tube to suck the blood out of my lungs. I couldn't breathe at all, then. When they did that, I fought them off because I thought it would kill me. I abused a top surgeon and punched a nurse in the throat.' She also convinced one of the nurses to give her a notepad, and wrote insulting notes to the staff. 'I was just so angry at being in this predicament,' says Samantha.

On Tuesday morning, at Samantha's insistence, the doctors removed the breathing tube. She had survived the lung haemorrhage. She was allowed to return to the ward wearing an oxygen mask. That night was an emotional turning point for Samantha. She left intensive care believing that she'd had to save herself, that she had survived through sheer willpower. She knew life would never be the same again. 'During that period in intensive care I realised what I could do for myself. It changed me. When the life support system was removed, I felt powerful, invincible. I had beaten death. I could do anything. I found out just how strong I could be.' It wasn't till months after her diagnosis that Samantha discovered how critical her leukaemia had been. Her family had been advised not to tell her, and she believes this was the right decision. 'If I had known exactly how bad I really was, I don't think I would have faced it the same way,' she recalls. 'At the time I thought the doctors had made a mistake and I had some weird stomach bug.' In fact, if she hadn't started treatment when she did, she would have been dead in three weeks.

Back in the ward, Samantha was given antibiotics and daily infusions of blood and platelets to boost her immune system. Though she'd beaten death, she was very weak, with severe diarrhoea and ulcers in her mouth and bowels. And if all that wasn't enough, her hair started to fall out. To raise her morale, her mother went out and bought her some hats and scarves to cover her head. Soon after, Samantha had the last of her hair shaved off.

Meanwhile, the news of Samantha's illness had spread, and she was inundated with cards and flowers. That cheered her up a little, but at the end of June she suffered another emotional blow. Reading through a nurse's study notes about leukaemia, she discovered that the treatment she was having could cause secondary cancers.

At the end of June, after her first course of chemotherapy, Samantha was allowed to go home. As she was highly susceptible to infection, she had to be kept in isolation — to her dismay, the family's two golden retrievers were banished from the house. Exhausted, she spent most of her days sitting in an armchair by the fire. An oncology nurse visited every day to check on her progress and help her inject herself with antibiotics through the Hickman line. Gradually her white-cell count increased, and her painful mouth ulcers disappeared.

Samantha returned to hospital a couple of weeks later for another bone-marrow biopsy, which showed that the cancer was in remission. They had beaten the disease back, at least for a while — she could go home again. To celebrate, her mother took her to the local shopping centre to buy a birthday present for a friend. But she felt uncomfortable when strangers stared at her, and was upset when some teenage girls laughed openly at her hat.

On 17 July she was well enough to go to Newcastle

to sit for an exam, but that night she became feverish and ill. This time it was pleurisy, a painful inflammation of the lining of the lungs. But she did not let that stop her enjoying a party with her family and friends on 18 July where everyone wore hats so Samantha would not feel different. Two days later she returned to hospital for her second course of chemotherapy.

This time Samantha's catheter was replaced with a new device about the size of a Walkman. Her drugs could be mixed, placed in a syringe and fed into this machine. She was finally free from the drip pole and could move around. Though the drugs caused constant nausea, she was allowed to go home again on 26 July.

By August, the effects of the second course of 'chemo' had kicked in. For two weeks Samantha suffered constant nausea and vomiting attacks, diarrhoea, heartburn, and severe head and body aches. Unable to bear the smell or sight of food, she subsisted on half a cracker, an icy pole or a little lemonade. She began to doubt she'd ever get well. 'I hated the chemotherapy,' she says. 'I hated how it made me feel like a wet string of spaghetti, exhausted and brain dead. I hated how I had to walk almost doubled over because my stomach was so sore from constant retching and heaving that I could not straighten up. I hated having to be lifted out of the bath and wiped dry as I crouched trembling on the floor, my limbs on the verge of collapse.' She was also fighting with her father, whose constant worrying drove her mad.

There was more to come. Later in the month, Samantha developed an allergy to one of her antibiotics, and her kidneys shut down; she had to be taken off all medication for a couple of weeks. Her appetite returned, but she found she could eat almost nothing because her stomach had shrunk. Desperate for a break, her parents took the family away for a holiday in the Hunter Valley.

On 15 September, three months after her diagnosis, Samantha turned 21, and celebrated with three parties. A week later, her third course of chemo

Samantha Miles on holiday in the Hunter Valley. Photo courtesy Samantha Miles.

began. This time she suffered a series of high fevers and teeth-rattling chills characteristic of chemo — the nurses called this 'shake and bake'. By October, Samantha was back at home and eating well, getting ready for the final stage of her treatment — a bone-marrow transplant. It was only then that the doctor told her about the risks involved in a bone-marrow transplant. She had only a one-in-three chance of surviving, he said, and even then there was only a fifty per cent chance that the transplant would succeed. Samantha was shocked: she hadn't realised how dangerous it was. But when she was given the choice of opting out of the treatment, she chose to go ahead. It was either a bone-marrow transplant or death, and Samantha very much wanted to live. As for side effects, the drugs were known to cause severe nausea, diarrhoea, vomiting, fevers, burning of the salivary glands and mouth ulcers — not to mention the possibility of contracting secondary cancers and ending up unable to have children. The prospect filled Samantha with dread.

When possible, bone marrow is taken from a close relative whose DNA is compatible. Unfortunately for Samantha, her sister's bone marrow was not a close enough match. She would have to have an 'autologous' transplant — that is, she would have to use her own bone marrow. The advantage of an autologous transplant was that, because the bone marrow had come from Samantha, her body would not reject it. The disadvantage was that the doctors could never be sure they'd destroyed every last vestige of leukaemia in the bone marrow before replacing it.

Early in December Samantha entered hospital for the first stage of her bone-marrow transplant. She was attached to a Cell Separator Unit, a machine which 'harvested' the stem cells from her blood. Next morning she went home. Then, on 14 December, she returned to hospital for the big operation. Under general anaesthetic, bone marrow was extracted from her hipbones with a wide-bore syringe. This is a brutal process. 'When I woke up from the general anaesthetic, I was in the worst physical pain I have ever experienced and bleeding badly,' recalls Samantha. 'It felt like a herd of elephants had just run over my back.' The bone marrow was then frozen and stored.

Before beginning a week of intensive chemotherapy, Samantha was placed on a saline drip to protect her kidneys from the chemicals. This time around, the chemo made her violently nauseous, hypersensitive to smells and touch, and destroyed her appetite. Strung out with anxiety, she scarcely slept for ten days. She became very emotionally vulnerable, and felt as if she were being treated as a 'case', not a person — that when the medical staff looked at her they saw only an illness, not a

Samantha Miles

frightened young woman. To cheer her up, her mother and sister brought in tinsel, tartan ribbon and a plastic Christmas tree. Samantha hung tinsel all over the room and stuck Christmas cards on the wall.

On 23 December, while everyone else in Sydney was out doing their Christmas shopping, a nurse wheeled in a machine that looked like a large fish tank — it turned out to be a heating unit. The bags of frozen bone marrow and stem cells were placed inside to thaw. Then the bags of marrow were attached to Samantha's Hickman line, and life-saving, pink bone marrow flowed through the transparent tube into Samantha's veins. Soon after, she began to twitch and shake. Every nerve in her body jangled. But after two bags of marrow and the first unit of stem cells had been transfused, her kidneys blocked, and the treatment had to be stopped. When her kidneys started working again the next day, the last of the stem cells were transfused.

On Christmas Day her family and some friends visited her in hospital, and she was allowed out for lunch. It was a muted celebration. Over the next couple of days Samantha's hair — which had grown back — fell out again, and she felt desperately ill. Though she was given antidepressants and sleeping pills, she jumped, twitched and hallucinated the nights away.

About a week after the transplant, Samantha

developed a sore throat. Soon she could not swallow her own saliva. It ran down her chin, thick, gluggy and putrid; the chemicals had burned out the lining of her digestive tract — from her mouth, through her throat and stomach, to her bowel — and her body was producing huge amounts of mucous to protect it. Watched over by her anxious mother, she lay awake all night dribbling into a washcloth. To ease the pain from ulcers on her mouth, lips and tongue, she began sipping, then guzzling, morphine. Then she had to endure shake and bake temperatures and projectile vomiting. New Year's Eve passed without a trace.

Then, on 9 January 1993, Samantha's white cell count reached the magic number that showed the bone-marrow transplant had succeeded. She was in

Samantha Miles with three of her nurses. l to r: Clare, Marilyn and Sharon.
Photo courtesy Samantha Miles.

remission. Exhausted from sleep deprivation, depression and toxic chemicals, Samantha went home. For the next few months she had to attend hospital for platelet and blood transfusions, which were gradually phased out.

But if the battle for survival was over, the war of recovery had only just begun. For a year now, Samantha's life had been on hold. What should she do now? One thing was certain — she would never go back to Newcastle. Though she'd kept up with the theory subjects in her design degree, she had not been able to complete the practical assignments. Eventually she withdrew from the course and took a year off.

That year was a steep learning curve. Samantha felt she was standing still while her friends were whizzing past with their lives — everyone seemed to be moving ahead except her. Determined not to waste any more time, she looked for a project to keep her occupied while she recovered, and eventually decided to write a book about her cancer experience. At first she kept the writing a secret, but when a publisher accepted some chapters, she wrote openly. Though she'd read voraciously since primary school, Samantha had always believed she was too lazy to write. But she soon discovered that she liked it and it was something she seemed to be able to do.

Yet though Samantha was slowly recovering physically, emotionally she was fragile. Believing she didn't need it, she had not sought counselling to help her come to terms with the trauma of the illness, and nobody in her family wanted to talk about what had happened. As Samantha's parents were away at work all day, and her sister was at university, she was left largely to her own devices. When she began to melt down, nobody noticed. 'It started off by being conscious of what I ate,' she explains. But by August 1994 Samantha was showing signs of anorexia. 'I was trying to be healthy. I was alone a lot, and I began exercising a lot. I got up early and rode my horse, then went for a swim, wrote for five hours, cooked dinner for the family, then took a one-hour walk.'

At the end of that year, Ron Miles took his wife and children on a motoring holiday in the United States. It was a disaster. Samantha was still angry with her father because she felt he had sided with the doctors too much during her illness, and had not supported her. Being cooped up together in the car increased the tension; they seldom spoke. Samantha scarcely ate, and the anorexia became full-blown. 'Food was a constant source of friction — what I could or would eat, and what I wouldn't,' she says. 'It must have been a nightmare for my family. I saw not eating much as a form of empowerment. It was part of how I was going to transform myself into something I had always wanted to be. It was my choice.' When they returned home, Samantha resumed her design degree at the University of Western Sydney. Though she wasn't sure she really wanted to do it, she felt she had to succeed. She also became addicted to exercising, and her weight dropped to 34 kilograms.

At the end of 1994, Samantha realised she was no longer interested in design. She applied to do a Master of Arts program in writing, and was accepted on the strength of her manuscript. Her book, *At Least It's Not Contagious*, was published in April 1995, and received good reviews. She did a publicity tour and become a minor celebrity. 'I learned so much about myself from writing that book,' she says. 'I discovered I could actually help others with cancer.'

In 1996 Samantha was awarded a Queens Trust scholarship to help her complete her thesis. She enjoyed her studies, and did well, graduating with distinction in 1997. She was a semi-finalist in the Young Australian of the Year awards in both 1996 and 1997. After graduating, she worked as a publishing assistant for a Sydney publishing house for two years, and then moved into editing jobs.

In films and on television, people survive accidents or disease and go blithely on with their lives. In reality, it's not that simple. A serious illness in a child can be very hard on family relationships. Six years after Samantha's leukaemia, the Miles family broke up. Her parents divorced, and her sister went overseas. 'It could never go back to the way it was before I got sick,' she says. 'My family was largely destroyed by what happened to me.'

In addition, Samantha's illness left her with physical and emotional problems that have taken her years to work through — some will never be solved. Her body is scarred from operations, and for almost five years she suffered from stomach problems, exacerbated by anorexia. Once long and thick, her hair is now thin and short. The emotional impact of the leukaemia was even worse than the physical consequences. 'I became paranoid about meeting people who didn't know what I'd been through,' she recalls. 'I couldn't bear to be in a room with cigarette smoke in it. I worried about being forced to eat food I knew my stomach couldn't tolerate. For a long time I was afraid to drive anywhere.' Her personality changed, too; she became outspoken and stood up for herself more. 'A lot of times after I got better, my parents and sister thought they didn't know me,' she says. 'I was different. They thought I'd got someone else's bone marrow.' But the most devastating after-effect of the illness — and one that time won't heal — is her inability to have children. 'It made me feel very lost and directionless,' she says. 'I've unconsciously taken on my parents' belief that having children is why we're here. And I felt, and still feel, that it is just another strike against me in finding a successful and long-lasting relationship.'

Samantha Miles on her horse, Mia. Photo courtesy Samantha Miles.

Eight years after surviving cancer, Samantha Miles feels as if she's finally coming to terms with what happened to her. Though she has to monitor what she eats, her weight stays at around 46 kilograms. She works full time and competes in equestrian events on the weekend. She has a group of terrific friends. In writing, she has found something she loves and is good at, and intends to write more. 'It's one of the ways I can continue to challenge myself,' she says. Now 29, she has enrolled in a

Bachelor in Counselling degree so she can help teenagers, particularly those with cancer. 'My cancer experience was more positive than negative,' she says. 'I learned so much from it. I'm sure that belief helped me survive.'

Susie Maroney

The Loneliness of the Long-distance Swimmer

Susie Maroney (right) and Stacey Thompson, a local student, lighting an Olympic cauldron at Cronulla during the Sydney 2000 Olympic Games. Photo courtesy *St George and Southern Shire Leader*.

Susie Maroney started swimming and winning marathons at 14. In the next ten years she set numerous records, and became the fastest woman to do a double crossing of the English Channel and the only person to swim from Cuba to Florida. At 25, she gave up ultra-marathon swimming.

Susie Maroney and her twin brother Sean were born on 15 November 1974 in the Sydney suburb of Kareela. They were the youngest of the five children of Pauline, a nurse, and Norm, an Assistant Commissioner in the New South Wales Police Service. Pauline, a severe asthmatic herself, introduced her children to swimming early to help control their asthma. As soon as they could stay afloat, Susie and Sean followed their older brothers and sisters, Michael, Karin and Lindy, into the pool, and before long Susie was doing laps with them.

The Maroneys are a competitive bunch, and by the time Susie turned 7, she was lining up to race at swimming carnivals. But competition swimming was not her forte. 'I competed in the pool and in distance events, but I got too nervous,' she recalls. 'I couldn't relax. I did better times in training than I could do in competition in the pool. I decided to see what would happen if I swam a marathon.'

There are three main ingredients for a successful career as a marathon athlete — the right genes, the right training program and the determination to stick at it. As it turned out, Susie Maroney had all of them. Her heart supplies lots of oxygen to her muscles and those muscles use it efficiently; she found a good trainer in Dick Caine; and she possessed the willpower and self-discipline to keep training through the pain and the boredom.

At 14, Susie swam her first marathon, a 16-kilometre race at the Manly Dam, and came second to the world champion. On the strength of that win, she was invited to join the Australian team that went to the 1989 US National Long Course Championship at Long Beach, California. Also on the team were two famous Australian distance swimmers — Shelley Taylor-Smith and Darren Turner — and Susie's big brother, Michael. Susie won the 25-kilometre swim, beating her older and more experienced team-mates.

Two weeks after her surprise victory, Susie competed in the annual 46-kilometre swim around New York's Manhattan Island, a charity event that raises money for the city's homeless children. Most of the field were experienced marathon swimmers in their late twenties; at 14, Susie was the youngest. 'For the first couple of kilometres it was like a washing machine,' she recalls. 'There were currents, dead rats, pieces of wood, even a dead giraffe from a zoo, at the start of the swim. The water was filthy. I got a shock.' And the homeless kids, instead of being grateful, stood on the bridges and threw rocks at the swimmers. Susie was the second woman across the finish line, and fourth overall.

The following year Susie returned to Manhattan. This time she outpaced the rest of the field, winning in a record time of seven hours seven seconds. It transformed her. 'I found something I was good at and that I enjoyed. If you do well, it makes you like what you're doing. Although I was in pain, it was a good kind of pain. You feel that you've really, really pushed all your muscles and haven't given up.'

Unlike pool swimming, marathon swimming does not have a calendar of events. Nor is it a Commonwealth or Olympic Games sport. The first problem Susie faced was finding opportunities to compete. She solved it by creating her own marathon events. The most obvious challenge was the English Channel, the Mount Everest of long-distance swimming. Not only is it the best-known long-distance swim in the world, it's also one of the toughest. The weather is changeable, the currents are swift, and it can get very cold in those choppy, green depths. Of more than 9000 people who have attempted it, only about 450 have succeeded. Susie decided to test her mettle on the Channel. 'I said to Mum, "I want to do it". She knew I was serious, and she supported me.'

Pauline Maroney set about organising a Channel swim for her daughter. Having never done anything like this before, she had to learn by experience. She started by ringing Des Renford, one of Australia's most prominent long-distance swimmers and a Channel veteran, for advice. Tapping away on her old manual typewriter, Pauline started contacting companies in Australia looking for sponsorship to help fund the swim. But as Susie was a newcomer to the sport, and as long-distance swimming isn't as popular or glamorous as Olympic swimming, the Maroneys had to find the money for Susie's Channel attempt themselves. The swim was planned for July 1990, the English summer.

Champion athletes seldom lead normal lives. For Susie, getting serious about long-distance swimming meant making sacrifices and developing iron self-discipline. Still in Year Ten at St Patrick's College in Sutherland, she went into training. Every morning she'd get up at dawn and plough up and down the pool from 5.30 a.m. till 8.00 a.m. After school, she'd be back in the pool from 3.30 p.m. till 6.30 p.m. 'Training every day was harder than the actual swims,' she recalls. 'I always had wet hair at school and no social life.' Saturdays would mean six hours straight, backwards and forwards across the bay at Coogee Beach. In the beginning she had company, but the other swimmers soon got bored and dropped away, leaving the bay to Susie. It was then that she began to appreciate just how lonely marathon swimming was going to be. 'It was winter, about fifteen degrees. Every Saturday, six hours, back and forth. I hated that. I was by myself, and it got boring.' To stay fit, Susie had to give up things most teenagers take for granted. 'All my friends were going to the beach, but I got too tired. And I only went to parties when there wasn't a big swim coming up.' There were compensations, however — travelling, belonging to an elite group of athletes, and mixing with people she found inspiring and interesting.

In July 1990 Pauline, Lindy and Michael accompanied Susie to England, where she went into training in Dover Harbour. She had plenty of company; there are always dozens of hopefuls trying to swim the Channel. They developed a sense of camaraderie in adversity. 'It was cold and painful, but we all enjoyed it because it was so tough,' she says.

At 6.30 a.m. on 31 July, jittery and excited, Susie stood on Dover Beach waiting to plunge into the sea. First, her mother slathered her with a mixture of beeswax, canola oil and Vaseline to help keep out the cold. Susie says her need for the grease is as much psychological as physical. 'It comes off after a few hours. It's disgusting when you put it on, but mentally it's essential. You think you'll be so much warmer. And it does help for the first few hours. It's a mind game, where every little bit of protection helps.'

At 7.00 a.m., buoyed by the best wishes of her little team, she waded into the English Channel. The sea was calm and flat at the start, but became choppy in the middle. Susie handled the turbulence easily. 'I didn't feel sick, and I didn't vomit. It was only in my later swims that I developed seasickness. Now, for every forty-five minutes I swim I'll vomit for five minutes.' The cold was another matter. 'It gets into your muscles. When you finally get to France, it's hard to stand up — and you have to stand on the shore to get the record.' Even then she realised how much success depended on mental attitude. 'It's all in your head,' she says. 'You can be a good swimmer and not make it.'

It took Susie eight hours and nineteen minutes to swim the 35 kilometres to Calais. At 15, she was the youngest Australian to swim the Channel, and set a new national record as well. It was a huge accomplishment, and she was proud of it. 'The Channel swim put me on the map,' she says.

Psychologically, that swim was a turning point for Susie Maroney; on the beach at Dover she'd found a role model. During training, she'd been watching a

Australian Heroines

Swimming the English Channel. Photo courtesy Susie Maroney.

young German woman called Inge getting ready for her swim. Inge, who had lost both legs in a farming accident, would take off her artificial legs and her coach would carry her across the pebbly beach to the water. She attempted the Channel the day after Susie, but ran out of steam after seventeen hours, just off the French coast. Undaunted, she vowed to come back every year till she made it. Inge's determination was inspiring. Sitting on the beach the day after her own swim, Susie decided that the Channel crossing had been too easy: she had to push herself to the limit, like Inge. What about a double crossing, she said to her mother. Over 400 people had swum the Channel, but only 15 had made it across and back.

The following July, Susie, now 16, returned to Dover. Her German friend was back, making another attempt. For the last two hours of the swim the cramp in Susie's right leg became so bad she could only kick with her left. Her sister, Lindy, who'd crossed in nine hours and forty-four minutes the day before, jumped off the support boat and swam the last 8 kilometres with her. Susie triumphed again, setting a world record of seventeen hours and fourteen minutes for the double crossing. This caught the attention of the English media, and when she dragged herself onto the pebbles at Dover, she was immediately surrounded by a gang of journalists and photographers. The next day the tabloids carried photos of Susie Maroney, marathon swimmer. The day after, Inge successfully completed the crossing, taking twenty-one hours to swim to France.

Susie was hooked. 'You get addicted to it and get competitive. You want to see how far you can go, but there are not that many marathon swims around. It's hard to find new ones.' In 1992 the Maroney family — including Pauline, who was then 50 — returned to Dover to swim a relay across the Channel. Unfortunately, Michael started to suffer from hypothermia because of the cold water, and the relay was called off. The next year they tried again, and made it.

Then, in 1993, after two years of research and months of preparation, Susie and her team flew to Cuba. Susie was going to attempt to swim 200 kilometres from Havana to Florida in the United States. Expected to take fifty hours, the swim was a quantum leap from anything Susie had done before. The fast-flowing Gulf Stream cuts across the route, and the warm waters are full of sharks, jellyfish and poisonous man-of-war stingers. Nobody had ever made this swim before. In recent times an American swimmer had tried it, but had dropped out after only two-and-a-half hours in the shark cage.

With Susie were her mother, who was going to monitor her health on the swim, and her brother Michael, a fireman and triathlete. As Susie's greatest supporter, Pauline Maroney has been central to her daughter's career as a marathon swimmer. 'Mum knows me better than everyone else. We're best friends. I wouldn't be able to do it without her. She knows if I'm okay or not.' Michael has been Susie's role model since she was a kid, and accompanies her on all her big swims. 'Michael and I are very close,' says Susie. 'He took me to New York and to Cuba. We clicked when I was very young because Michael was a good swimmer and good at triathlon. He's a fanatical trainer.'

To help her prepare, Susie had swum 94 kilometres in a Sydney pool in twenty-four hours, in the process setting a record for the *Guinness Book of Records*. 'In my head I wanted to know if I could do twenty-four hours,' she recalls. 'Till then I'd only done seventeen hours in the double Channel crossing. Mentally, I needed to get into the twenties.'

But the prospect of staying in the water for fifty hours was a lot more daunting than twenty-four. 'People told me that if I used the current correctly, I could go slow and take forty to fifty hours to get there,' Susie says. 'But I didn't want to hear that it would take that long. It depressed me.'

Problems dogged the operation from the beginning. There was debate about the route Susie should swim — a direct route across the Gulf Stream or a longer route which avoided the Gulf Stream currents. Susie ended up taking the advice of Gerry, the Cuban captain of the boat that would accompany her. He recommended the direct route. 'I trusted him,' Susie says. Besides, the prospect of swimming an extra 10 kilometres had frightened her. 'I go crazy if I think I have to swim 10 kilometres more.'

There was also a question mark over the shark-proof cage, which had been built in the United States and delivered sight unseen to Havana. It had been designed to be towed behind the boat, but Susie wanted it attached to the side, so she could be in constant contact with her mother and brother. To add to the tension, a documentary team was filming the swim. Susie tried to keep calm. 'It was the scariest swim I'd ever done,' she says. 'When I pictured forty hours in the water in my head, I got so scared. And it showed.'

Bad weather set in for four days, delaying the swim. With the money running out, the pressure began to mount in the Maroney camp. Susie developed her own strategies to stay sane. 'At night I pictured the worst things that could happen. Could I handle the jellyfish? But I didn't think about it too much because I'd worry. I'd say to myself, "What's two days? After that I can have a break and eat a burger. No matter what, it will have to be over. This can't last forever." I used to go for walks by myself. You couldn't talk to anyone about it because people simply didn't understand. It hadn't been done before.'

Finally the weather cleared, and just after four o'clock on the morning of Saturday 8 June 1996, in front of a crowd of Cuban well-wishers including the Mayor, Susie Maroney dived into Havana Harbour, swam out to the boat and climbed into the cage, which was now attached to the boat's side. Accompanying their boat was a cruiser belonging to Susie's American sponsor. On it was the official observer who would declare the swim a success or a failure — Tom Hetzell, president of the Marathon Swimming Association. Excited, nervous and scared, Susie had to stop herself from sprinting. It was essential that she pace herself or she'd quickly run out of steam.

Almost immediately the boat ran into an east wind. It whipped up the sea and caused turbulence in Susie's cage, making her horribly seasick. For six long hours the wind kept up. By then Susie was becoming severely dehydrated from the vomiting. Pauline tried to keep her fluids up and fed her yogurt, but Susie could not keep anything in her stomach. Meanwhile, the sea on the other side of the boat was calm. Worried about her health, her sponsor talked her into swimming outside the cage for an hour in the calm water. The crew on both boats watched for sharks. That break probably saved the swim: Susie got into a rhythm and started to recover.

Susie had been swimming for about fourteen hours now. Her arms were dead, her throat and tongue were swollen and sore from the salt water, and every minute seemed like an hour. 'When you dive in you feel so excited because it's finally going to happen,' she explains. 'The first eight hours go so fast. But when you start getting towards fourteen hours and it starts to get dark, you feel like you'll never get there. Especially when you can't see land.' At times like these, it's essential to Susie to have people on the boat who care about her. 'It's good to have your family there because you can scream at them,' she says.

During the long swim, Susie sometimes concentrated on her swimming, and at other times seemed to be in a dream. Marathon swimmers use this mechanism of 'association' and 'dissociation' to cope with the boredom and pain. When they're in their body, they monitor their stroke and breathing, and correct their technique to get the best possible performance. When they can't take any more of this, they forget their body, go into automatic pilot, and daydream. This lets them forget the stings, the soreness, the seasickness for a while.

When it grew dark, Susie got spooked and went back into the cage, unwilling to put herself at risk in the open sea. 'I had little fluorescent sea creatures in the cage. I was in my own little world. I thought the cage was my swimming pool.' But she soon came back to earth when sea lice stung her all over her body. 'They got all down my cossie and all over my face, but at least something happened to take my mind off the hours I still had to swim.' After being stung, she put on a rash vest — a lycra bodysuit. Then early in the morning, when the water cooled down, she began to shiver. As shivering wastes precious energy and plays havoc with swimming technique, she had to get warm. At 3.00 a.m. Susie struggled into her wetsuit. Later, she would discover that the wetsuit had chafed her skin badly, but at the time she was oblivious. 'At that stage, when I was dying, it didn't really hurt,' she explains. 'You can't feel how much it's hurting you till you get out.'

In the middle of the night a storm blew up. Lightning flashed and the seas topped 2 metres. It lasted six hours. On the boat, Pauline and Michael became dreadfully seasick. In the cage, Susie was struggling. After twenty-six hours in the water, she'd swum 110 kilometres, and had over fifty to go. By now, she was mentally and physically exhausted and had severe pain in her shoulders. And with her normal body rhythms upset, she was sleepy and depressed. She was also hallucinating. 'I was seeing crocodiles in the cage and thought they were going to attack each other. I saw monkeys on the cage, and Santa Claus on the boat.' Hallucinations are the body's way of protecting itself, a mental version of the shock response one experiences after an accident. It gives you a break before the pain hits. But still Susie swam.

After thirty-nine hours in the water, Susie hit the wall. She felt as if she was going backwards. 'There was a strong current. I decided it was enough to get into American waters. I'd had enough. I was disoriented, not thinking. I was really tired. My body was meant to be asleep. I was exhausted and cold.' Michael and Pauline tried to decide whether to let her continue or call off the swim. At feeding stops, they told Susie she had another 20 kilometres to go

Australian Heroines

Susie Maroney with her twin brother Sean, during the Cuba–US swim in 1993. Photo courtesy Susie Maroney.

to reach land. What did she want to do? But by now Susie was beyond rational thought; questions just made her angry. 'I just wanted to get there the quickest way possible,' she says. 'After thirty-seven hours, if they start talking about just another 20 kilometres, you think: "That's another marathon!" All I wanted to hear was that I only had 500 metres to go.'

When Susie reached US waters, Pauline and Michael decided she'd had enough. They radioed the official observer, who came aboard and called off the swim. When they pulled Susie out of the water, she was a physical wreck, howling with emotion, exhaustion and pain. 'It took me two months to recover physically,' she says. 'I had stress fractures on my wrists and ankles. My wrists are narrow and just hitting the waves all the time hurts them, but you can't strap them up for swimming. My face was puffy and my stomach covered in itchy bites. The worst thing was being itchy. But you don't really care because you're so happy to be out of the water.' She was taken to hospital, where it was revealed she'd lost 11 kilograms, and had huge angry blisters all over her body from chafing.

As a super-fit athlete, Susie recovered from the physical stress of the Cuba swim relatively quickly. But mentally it took her a long time to get over it. 'I suffered so much. It makes me appreciate that swim. It was the toughest I've ever done. I'll always remember it.'

Though Susie Maroney had not reached American soil, she'd swum 160 kilometres, only 20 kilometres short of the US coast, and had remained in the water for thirty-seven hours. After the swim, some Australian sports commentators implied that she had got too much help from the cage, that it had pulled her along. Pauline tried to shield Susie from the knockers, but of course she heard the criticisms. She was hurt, and still believes the swim was a major achievement. 'I knew in my heart that swimming for 37 hours was a lot.' In fact, much of Susie's pain could have been avoided. The US Coast Guard later sent the Maroneys a map showing that the boat captain had strayed 25 kilometres off course during the storm. If he had stayed on course, Susie would have landed on Florida's Key West beach in the twenty-ninth hour of her swim.

But near enough would never be good enough for Susie Maroney. In May 1997 the Maroneys were back in Havana for another attempt at the Cuba–US super-marathon. This time, assisted by a northerly current, Susie made it to Key West in twenty-four hours and thirty-one minutes, becoming the first person to complete the swim. She became a media sensation in the US, and appeared on the David Letterman television show with the actor Helen Hunt. She was also featured in *Vogue* and *Sports Illustrated* magazines.

After her second swim, Susie met the Communist Cuban leader, Fidel Castro, who treated the family to a four-and-a-half-hour banquet. 'He was everything I'd expected,' she says. 'I'd read about him. He was so warm. I couldn't stop looking at him. He was tall, had a beard, was charismatic. He asks so many questions; he's so intelligent.' What Susie didn't realise was that she had inadvertently swum into deep political waters. When her meeting with Castro was leaked to the press, anti-Communist Cuban refugees in Florida created a furore, accusing her of giving good publicity to a communist regime. Susie is unrepentant. 'I'm not political. I'm just a swimmer.

Susie Maroney

I only did the Cuba–US swim because it was the right stretch of water.'

Fidel Castro proved to be a good friend. On learning that Susie was planning a marathon from Mexico to Cuba, he promised to pay the Maroney team's accommodation and mooring fees in Havana. In 1998, Susie swam the 179 kilometres from Mexico to Cuba in thirty-nine hours, the longest non-stop ocean swim on record. The following year, on her final supermarathon, she swam from Jamaica to Cuba in twenty-seven hours.

Susie Maroney was a success: she'd logged up three world records in supermarathon swimming in as many years. But it was too much, too soon. When Susie was 16, her coach, Dick Caine, had resigned because he thought she was pushing herself too hard, and risked burning out and doing long-term damage. Susie hadn't listened then — as her mother says, 'How do you stop a freight train?' — but nine years later, it looked as if he'd been right. The pace was becoming unsustainable. When she wasn't training, she was in the sea trying to break records for long-distance swimming, or trying to raise money for the next swim. Susie began to wilt under her own expectations, the demands of her sponsors, and the appearances for the numerous charities she supported. Something had to give.

Only weeks after she returned from Cuba in 1999,

Susie's life began to career out of control. 'I was so tired from the Jamaica–Cuba swim and my grandmother died as soon as we got back,' she recalls. 'And I still had an eight-hour charity swim to do. I'd also broken up with my first-ever boyfriend. I needed a break, but I didn't know how to say it. There's the constant pressure of what you are doing next. When you've got sponsors you can't pull out.' She started to lose her grip.

Pauline Maroney became worried. 'Susie was crying a lot. It was hard to know what to do. The family was saying slow down and take a year off, but she couldn't see it herself. Everything came together at one time, and tipped her over the edge.'

On Saturday 30 October 1999, Susie swam 675 laps of the pool at the Cook and Phillip Aquatic Centre in Sydney. Later that night, some friends took her to a nightclub to cheer her up. But when Susie left around 1.00 a.m., she was still depressed. She couldn't sleep, and could not call her mother, who was working the night shift at Sutherland Hospital, for help. Early in the morning of 31 October, Susie suffered a mental and physical breakdown.

Susie spent a week in hospital recuperating and having some counselling. 'I'm glad it happened,' she says now. 'I would have cracked up some other time. I needed to stop and talk to people not associated with swimming so they could tell me I was okay. It

Susie Maroney

stopped some of the demands.' Since then, Susie has been taking a break. 'It's taken her months to learn to unwind,' says her mother. 'She'd feel guilty because she wasn't training. She'd jump up and run down to the beach and do a few laps in the sea.'

Now Susie only trains when she feels like it. 'I'm starting to enjoy it again because I don't have to do it,' she admits. She is continuing her work for the charities she supports — the Asthma Foundation, the Leukaemia Foundation, the Paralympics, and Young at Heart Cardiac Research are some of them. 'I'd like to do one more swim for a charity I believe in,' she says. 'Not necessarily a long swim — I've done them all.' And she has to earn a living. Although she's been showered with honours — an Order of Australia, Australian Young Achiever of the Year, New South Wales Woman of the Year — and was appointed to the Swimming Hall of Fame in Florida, marathon swimming has not made Susie rich. She's philosophical about her choices, though. 'It's not popular, it's not supported, but I've enjoyed it. I was never in it as a job, anyway. I can get by, but I could never retire.

'I love to travel, and I'd like to work in the travel industry. The family have been supporting me for so long, but they've got to have their lives, too.' In the meantime, she was an ambassador at the 2000 Sydney Olympics, meeting and greeting athletes at the Olympic Village and helping them to feel at home, and she ran in the Olympic torch relay.

By giving up marathon swimming, Susie Maroney has lost something that consumed every waking hour for nearly ten years. Now she has to find another identity for herself, and this could prove much harder, and take much longer, than swimming from Cuba to Florida. Athletes who give up their sport experience a kind of death, and have to work their way through a form of grieving. But Susie is determined to make the transition from water to dry land. 'I don't want to grow old still doing competitive swimming,' she says. 'I want the choice.'

Glossary

Bloomers: knee-length winter knickers with elastic in the legs
Bullseyes: red-and-white-striped boiled sweets
Cutter: a small boat carried by a large ship
Gunyah: a temporary shelter for Aborigines, usually made from a frame of branches covered with bark, leaves or grass
Mia-mia: a rough shelter made of tree branches or bark; invented by the Aborigines and copied by the white settlers
Pogrom: an organised massacre, especially of Jews
Squatters and selectors: squatters were people who had settled on public land to which they had no legal title. Most were in the wool industry. After 1836 they were granted grazing rights for an annual fee. The Gold Rushes of the 1850s brought an influx of people wanting to farm the land. Reacting to this pressure the New South Wales government passed a law in 1861, opening up the land to these new, small landholders, or selectors.
Tender: a vessel which provides stores or carries passengers or orders for a larger ship
Ticket-of-leave: the certificate given to a convict once he or she had served all or part of their sentence. It excused them from compulsory labour and allowed them to choose their employer and work for wages. It was usually granted for good behaviour.
Transported: convicts were sent from England by ship to the Australian colonies to serve out their jail sentences
Windlass: a simple machine with a handle to turn for hauling or hoisting heavy loads with minimum effort

Sources

Mary Bryant

Applin, Graeme (ed) (1988) *A Difficult Infant: Sydney Before Macquarie*, UNSW Press, Sydney.

Barton, G B (1889) *History of New South Wales from Records, Vol I — Governor Phillip 1783–1789*, NSW Government Printer, Sydney.

Becke, Louis & Jeffery, Walter (1896) *A First Fleet Family: A Hitherto Unpublished Narrative of Certain Remarkable Adventures Compiled from the Papers of Sergeant William Dew of the Marines*, T Fisher Unwin, London.

Bladen, F M (ed) (1893) *Historical Records of New South Wales, Vol II — Grose and Paterson 1793–1795*, New South Wales Government Printer, Sydney.

Clune, F (1940) *To the Isles of Spice*, Angus & Robertson, Sydney.

Currey, C H (1983) (1963) *The Transportation, Escape and Pardoning of Mary Bryant*, Halstead Press, Sydney.

Donkin, Nance (1982) 'First Fleet Marriages', *This Australia*, Vol 1, No. 4.

Holden, Robert (2000) *Orphans of History: The Forgotten Children of the First Fleet*, Text Publishing, Melbourne.

Martin, James (1938) *Memorandoms* (sic), edited by Charles Blount, Rampart Lions Press, London.

Newgate Calendar, 'Nathaniel Lilley, James Martin, Mary Briant (sic), William Allen and John Butcher: Convicted of Returning from Transportation', Vol 3, 1824–1828, London.

Pottle, F A (1938) *Boswell and the Girl from Botany Bay*, William Heinemann Ltd, London.

Sources

Rawson, Geoffrey (1938) *The Strange Case of Mary Bryant*, Angus & Robertson, Sydney.

Robinson, Portia (1988) *The Women of Botany Bay*, The Macquarie Library, Sydney.

Tench, Watkin (1961) *Sydney's First Four Years: Being a Reprint of a Narrative of the Expedition to Botany Bay and a Complete Account of the Settlement at Port Jackson*, edited by L F Fitzhardinge, Library of the Australian Historical Society in association with the Australian Historical Society.

Molly Craig

Gardiner-Garden, John (9 June 1999) *From Dispossession to Reconciliation*, Research Paper 27 1998–99, Parliamentary Library, Canberra.

Haebich, Anna (1988) *For Their Own Good: Aborigines and Government in the South-west of Western Australia 1900–1940*, University of Western Australia Press, Perth.

Hasluck, Paul (1970) *Black Australians: A Survey of Native Policy in Western Australia 1829–1897*, 2nd edn, Melbourne University Press.

Human Rights and Equal Opportunity Commission (April 1997) *Bringing them Home: Report of the National Inquiry into the Separation of Aboriginal and Torres Strait Island Children from their Families*, Commonwealth of Australia, Canberra.

Maushart, Susan (1993) *Sort of a Place Like Home: Remembering the Moore River Native Settlement*, Fremantle Arts Centre Press, South Fremantle.

Pilkington, Doris /Garimara, Nugi (1996) *Follow the Rabbit-Proof Fence*, University of Queensland Press, St Lucia.

Rowley, C D (1971) *Outcasts in White Australia: Aboriginal Policy and Practice, Vol II*, Australian National University Press, Canberra.

Van den Berg, Rosemary (1994) *No Options, No Choice: The Moore River Experience*, Magabala Books, Broome.

Wagland, David (1996) *Ancient Mountains and Desert Sands: Impressions of the Inland Pilbara*, Yarra Publications, Mount Victoria.

Wells, A G (1982) *The Wild Pilbara: Iron Country and its Natural Wonders*, The Jaycees Community Foundation Inc, Perth.

Susie Maroney

Interviews with Susie & Pauline Maroney

Interview with Kenneth Graham & Dr Michael Martin, sports physiologists & John Crampton, Athlete Management Services, NSW Institute of Sport

Newspaper and magazine reports

BoB and FFC Pictures, (1996) *Susie is a Fish*, video produced by Judi McCrossin, written and directed by Carla Drago.

Samantha Miles

Interview with Samantha Miles

Miles, Samantha (1995) *At Least It's Not Contagious: A Personal Story of a Struggle with Leukaemia*, Allen & Unwin, Sydney.

— (2000) 'Topic of Cancer', in *Good Weekend*, 29 January.

Brigitte Muir

Interview with Brigitte Muir

Blum, Arlene (1984) *Annapurna: A Woman's Place*, Granada, London.

Hillary, Sir Edmund (1999) *View from the Summit*, Doubleday, London.

Sources

Muir, Brigitte (1998) *The Wind in my Hair*, Viking, Ringwood Victoria.

Sarah White Musgrave

Bayley, William A (1956) *Rich Earth: History of Young and the Shire of Burrangong, New South Wales*, Young Municipal Council and Burrangong Shire Council.

Holland, Lyster (1985) *As it was in the Beginning*, Young District Historical Society.

Keesing, Nancy (1963) *By Gravel and Gum: The Story of a Pioneer Family*, Macmillan & Co Ltd, Melbourne.

Musgrave, Sarah (1984) *The Wayback*, 5th edn, The Bland Historical Society & the Young Historical Society.

Rolls, Eric (1993) *Sojourners*, University of Queensland Press, St Lucia.

Scott, Ernest (ed) (1929) *Australian Discovery, Vol II: By Land*, JM Dent & Sons Ltd/EP Dutton, London & New York.

Barbara Thompson

Bassett, Jan (ed) (1996) *Great Explorations: An Australian Anthology*, Oxford University Press Australia, Melbourne.

Bassett, Marnie (1966) *Behind the Picture: HMS Rattlesnake's Australia-New Guinea Cruise 1846 to 1850*, Oxford University Press, Melbourne.

Beale, Edgar (1970) *Kennedy of Cape York*, Rigby, Melbourne.

Huxley, Julian (ed) (1935) *T H Huxley's Diary of the Voyage of HMS Rattlesnake*, Chatto and Windus, London.

Lee, Sidney (ed) (1893) *Dictionary of National Biography*, Vol XXXV, MacCarwell-Maltby, Smith, Elder and Co.

— (1901) *Dictionary of National Biography*, Suppl Vol 1, Abbott-Childers, Smith, Elder and Co.

MacGillivray, John (1852) *Narrative of the Voyage of HMS Rattlesnake, Commanded by the Late Captain Owen Stanley, RN, FRS etc. During the Years 1846–1850: Including the Discoveries and Surveys in New Guinea, The Louisiade Archipelago, etc: To Which is Added the Account of Mr R B Kennedy's Expedition for the Exploration of the Cape York Peninsula*, Vol 1, T & W Boone, London.

Marshall, A J (1970) *Darwin and Huxley in Australia*, Hodder & Stoughton, Sydney.

Moore, David R (1979) *Aborigines and Islanders at Cape York: An Ethnographic Reconstruction Based on the 1848–1850 'Rattlesnake' Journals of O. W. Brierly and Information He Obtained from Barbara Thompson*, Australian Institute of Aboriginal Studies, Canberra/Humanities Press Inc., New Jersey.

Truganini

Barnard, James (1890) 'Aborigines of Tasmania', Reprinted from the *Transactions of the Australasian Society for the Advancement of Science Meeting*, Melbourne.

Roth, H Ling (1899) *The Aborigines of Tasmania*, 2nd edn, F King, Halifax.

Plomley, N J B (ed) (1966) *Friendly Mission: The Tasmanian Journals and Papers of George Augustus Robinson 1829–1834*, Tasmanian Historical Research Association.

Pybus, Cassandra (1991) *Community of Thieves*, William Heinemann Australia, Port Melbourne.

Rae Ellis, Vivienne (1981) *Trucanini: Queen or Traitor?*, Australian Institute of Aboriginal Studies, Canberra.

Reynolds, Henry (1995) *Fate of a Free People*, Penguin, Melbourne.

Rintoul, Stuart (1993) *The Wailing: A National Black Oral History*, William Heinemann Australia, Melbourne.

Sources

Roberts, Jan (1986) *Jack of Cape Grim: A Victorian Adventure*, Greenhouse Publications, Richmond.

Robinson, George Augustus, 'Australian Aborigines Protection Society: A portion of the report of the meeting of October 19, 1838', reprinted from *The Colonist*, 31 October 1838, Noyes & Son.

Ryan, Lyndall (1996) *The Aboriginal Tasmanians*, 2nd edn, University of Queensland Press, St Lucia.

Marika Weinberger

Interviews with Marika Weinberger

Biderman, Abraham H (1995) *The World of My Past*, Random House Australia, Sydney.

Calvocoressi, Peter, Wint, Guy & Pritchard, John (1972, 1989) *The Penguin History of the Second World War*, Penguin Books, London.

Gutman, Yisrael & Berenbaum, Michael (eds) (1994) *Anatomy of the Auschwitz Death Camp*, Indiana University Press, Bloomington & Indianapolis, Published in association with the United States Holocaust Memorial Museum, Washington DC.

Levi, Primo (1997) 'Survival in Auschwitz', in Jean E Brown, Elaine C Stephens & Janet E Kugin (eds) *Images from the Holocaust: A Literature Anthology*, NTC Publishing Group, Lincolnwood, Illinois.

Marton, Kati (1982) *Wallenberg: Missing Hero*, Arcade Publishing, New York.

Speigelman, Art (1987) *Maus I: A Survivor's Tale*, Penguin Books, London.

— (1991) *Maus II: And Here My Troubles Began*, Penguin Books, London.

Sydney Jewish Museum: *A Museum of Australian Jewish History and the Holocaust, A Publication to mark the opening of the Museum on 18 November, 1992.*

Weinberger, Marika (21 June 1995) interviewed by Rosemary Block for the *Survivors of the Shoah*, Visual History Foundation, Videotapes I & II, Sydney.

May Wirth

Greaves, Geoff (1980) *The Circus Comes to Town*, Reed Books, Melbourne.

Ramsland, John with Mark St Leon (1993) *Children of the Circus: The Australian Experience*, Butterfly Books, Springwood.

Cheong, C H (1930) 'Transporting a Circus' in *Wirth Bros Ltd Circus Menagerie: Greatest Show on Earth*, Past Review and Program.

King, M (1990) *The Silver Road: The Life of Mervyn King, Circus Man, as told to Mr St Leon*, Butterfly Books, Springwood.

St Leon, Mark (1983) 'World Famous Equestrienne: Australia's May Wirth,' *This Australia*, Vol 3, No. 4, pp 57–61.

— (1995) 'May Wirth' in *Companion to Theatre in Australia*, Philip Parsons, (gen ed) Currency Press/Cambridge University Press, Sydney.

— (1995) 'Circus,' in *Companion to Theatre in Australia*, Philip Parsons, (gen ed) Currency Press/Cambridge University Press, Sydney.

— (1984) *Australian Circus Reminiscences*, Self-published, Ultimo.

— (1990) *The Bareback Queen: The Story of May Wirth*, unpublished manuscript, Mitchell Library, State Library of New South Wales.

Index

Page numbers in *italics* refer to photographs

Aaron (guide), 227, *228*
Aboriginal and Torres Strait Islander Commission, 161, 163
Aboriginal Arts Board, 163
Aborigines
   assimilation policy, 132, 158–9, 160, 165
   attack Mary Bryant's party, 14, 15
   Cape York, 75
   conflict with whites, 156
   deaths in custody, 163
   forced into settlements and missions, 157–8
   given vote in 1967 referendum, 162
   government Boards of Protection, 158
   'half-castes', 132, 155, 160
   human dragnet to drive out, 42
   land rights, 162–4
   massacre of Pennemukeer people, 40
   New South Wales, 84, 90–3, 158–9
   Northern Territory, 158–9
   Pilbara region, 153–5
   political activism, 60, 160–2
   Queensland, 159
   reconciliation march, 165
   remains of in museums, 59–60
   removal of children from parents, 132–3, 156–65
   Robinson's 'Friendly Mission' to, 31, 35–45, 53
   South Australia, 159
   Tasmania, 31–6, 40–4, 46, 52, 56–60
   Victoria, 46–51, 159
   Western Australia, 132–3, 153–9, 159, 161
   witness First Fleet arrive, 7
   see also Torres Strait Islanders
Aburda (Aborigine), 74–5
Aconcagua, 223
Adams, James, 79
Adventure Plus, 225
Alikia (Aborigine), 68, 72, 78
Allen, William, 12, 19
altitude sickness, 219–20
America (ship), 65
Ann and Elizabeth (ship), 22
anti-Semitism, 168–71, 173–4, 179, 203–10
   see also concentration camps
Arthur, George, 35, 42, 43
Aschheim, Irma, 175
Aschheim, Josef, 170
Atlas, Joly, 189–90, *191*
Auschwitz concentration camp, 173, 179–86, 207, *207*, 208
Australian Aboriginal League, 161
Australian Association of Jewish Holocaust Survivors, 200

Australian Institute of Aboriginal
  Studies, 163
Axis, 205

Babette (Marika Weinberger's
  friend), 193, 198
Badulaig people, 71
Barbara (prison guard), 190
Baring (ship), 107
Barnum and Bailey Circus, 109,
  119–20, 124
Barton, George, 25
Bass, Dick, 217
Batavia, 18
Baudin, Nicolas, 56
Beaumont, Dezeppo Marie, 109
Bentham, Jeremy, 26
Bergen-Belsen concentration
  camp, 208
Bergida, Judy, 171, *173*, 177,
  187, 189
Black Line, 42
The Bland (station), 95–8
Bligh, William, 18, 56
Blount, Charles, 26
Boroto (Aborigine), 68, 72, 78
Boswell, James, 2, 21–2, 26, 27, 29
Botany Bay, 6
Bounty (ship), 18
Bramble (ship), 61
Brierly, Oswald, 73, 77, 78–9, 80
Brisbane, 63
Broad, Dolly, 22, 26
Broad, Mary *see* Bryant, Mary
Bryant, Emanuel, 10, 12, 13, 16,
  18, 24, 25
Bryant, Mary, 2–29
  early life, 2–3
  as a convict, 3–8
  escapes from custody, *1*, 12–16
  recaptured, 18–20
  Boswell takes up cause of, 21–3

researching the life of, 24–9
Bryant, William, 4, 8, 11–16,
  18, 24–8
Buchenwald concentration camp,
  204, 208
Burrangong (station), 85–95,
  98–100, 102
Burrowmunditroy, 84–5
bushrangers, 86–8, 103–4
Butcher, John, 12

Caine, Dick, 265, 281
Canning Stock Route, 154
Carr, Mr (overseer), 96–7
Carralup Settlement, 132
Castro, Fidel, 280–1
cerebral oedema, 226
Charlotte (ship), 5–6, 20, 24, 25
Chinese, in Australia, 100–1
Cierer, Edita, 166, 168
  at school, 167
  decides to stay with sister, 176
  in Auschwitz, 180–2, 183–4
  in Kaiserwald, 187–9
  in Stutthof, 190
  in Glöwen, 192–3
  in Ravensbrück, 194
  in Malchov, 195
  settles in Australia, 200
  death, 201
Cierer, Henrik, 174, 197–8
Cierer, Irena, 167, 168, 174,
  189, 197
Cierer, Omama, 174, 175
Cierer, Peter, 174, 175, 197
Cierer, Vojtech, 167, 168, 169–71,
  174, 176, 180, 197
circuses, 109–10, 127
Cirque of the Unclimbables,
  214–15, *215*
Cobborn Jackie, 84, 85, 89, 92, 93
Colebrook, 159

Index

Coll, John, 227, 228
Colleano, Con, 127
Colleano, Winnie, 127
Collins, David, 34
concentration camps
  Auschwitz, 173, 179–86, 207, 207, 208
  Bergen-Belsen, 208
  Buchenwald, 204, 208
  Dachau, 203
  Flossenburg, 204
  Glöwen, 191–3
  Kaiserwald, 186–9
  Majdanek, 208
  Malchov, 195
  Mauthausen, 204
  Ravensbrück, 193–5, 204
  Sachenhausen, 204
  Stutthof, 190–1
convicts, 3–7, 9, 10–12, 24, 63, 107
Cook, James, 56
Cooke, John Welby, 115
Council for Aboriginal Reconciliation, 163
Council of Aboriginal Affairs, 162
Cox, James, 4, 12, 19, 24
Cox, William, 106
Craig, Maude, 130
Craig, Molly, *129*, 130–52
  early childhood, 131–2
  removed from parents, 133–6
  at Moore River Native Settlement, 136–41
  escapes from Moore River, 142, 151
  walks back to Jigalong, 143–9, *150*
  marries, 151
Craig, Thomas, 130
Cross, Harry, 151
Currey, Charles, 26–7, 28
Curriberrima (station), 102

Dachau concentration camp, 203
Dandridge, John, 54–5
Davenport, Orrin, 121
de Mott, Josie, 118, 124
Dean, Tommy, 112, 117, 119, 121
Denali, 221–2
D'Entrecasteaux, Joseph Antoine, 56
Despoges, John, 109
Dorje (Sherpa), 235
Dray (Aborigine), 33, 34, 36, 39, 43, 45
Duff, Mal, 234
Dunkirk (prison hulk), 4

East Perth Girls' Home, 136
Eden, Anthony, 207
Edwards, Edward, 18, 19, 24
Eichmann, Adolf, 209
Eroni Brothers Circus, 110

Fanny (Aborigine), 48, 49, 50
Federal Native Title Act 1993, 164
Fields, Gracie, 130–4, 136, 139, 141, 144–5, 148, 151
First Fleet, 5, 24
Fisher, Scott, 232, 233
Flanagan, Mrs, 146
Flinders Island, 43, 45–6, 51
Flossenburg concentration camp, 204
Fowey, 22–3, 28, 29
Friendly Mission, 31, 35–45, 53
Frinda (Aborigine), 134
From, Fred, 217
Fryer, Catherine, 3

Gangotri, 218
Gardiner, Frank, 103
gas chambers, 182, 186, 208
Gasherbrum Two, 219–21
Gdansk, 190

295

Germany, in World War II, 203–10
Gilbert (bushranger), 103, 104
Glatz, Konrad, 174, 176
Glöwen concentration camp, 191–3
Goering, Hermann, 209
gold rushes, 93–4, 99–101, 102–3
Gorgon (ship), 19–20, 25
Gran Paradiso, Italy, 214
Groves, George, 88, 98
Grunstein, Stephen, 179, 197
Grynszpan, Herschel, 203
Guardian (ship), 10
Gumakudin people, 71
Gunage (Aborigine), 70, 74, 78
Gurindji people, 162

Half-Caste Institution, Alice Springs, 159
Hall, Rob, 232, 233
Hawke government, 163
Haydon, Mary, 3
head-hunting, 71
Hetzell, Tom, 274
Heydrich, Reinhardt, 205, 209
Hidden Peak, Karakorum, 218
Hillary, Edmund, 218
Hillary, Peter, 218
Himmler, Heinrich, 206, 208, 209
Hitler, Adolf, 169, 203, 208
Holocaust, 170–1, 201–2, 205–10
Holt government, 162
Hoornwey (ship), 19
Horssen (ship), 19
Höss, Rudolf, 208, 209
Hovell, William, 106
Hume, John, 88
Hungary, 169, 173
Hunt Brothers Circus, 127
Hunt, Helen, 280
Huxley, Thomas, 73, 78, 79, 80

Inge (swimmer), 269, 271
Israel, 210

Japan, in World War II, 205, 209
Jeanneret, Henry, 51
Jewish Museum, Sydney, 200, 202
Jews *see* anti-Semitism
Jigalong, 130–2, 152
Joe (horse), 118, 121
Jones, Martha, 139, 140, 142
Justinian (ship), 11

Kadibil, Daisy, 130–3, 136, 139, 141, 145, 147–8, 152
Kaiserwald concentration camp, 186–9
Kalundi Seventh Day Adventist Mission, 152
Kassa, 169
Kaurareg people, 68, 70–1, 72, 74, 76, 77–8, 81
Keeling, Mr (Protector of Aborgines), 131–2
Kelly, Annabelle, 151
Kelly, Doris, 151, 152
Kelly, Toby, 151
Kipa (Sherpa), 235
Kitty (horse), 122–3
Koch, Brigitte *see* Muir, Brigitte
Koch, Veronique, 217
Koolinda (ship), 135
Kosice, 167, 169, 198
Kristallnacht, 203–4

Labillardière, Captain, 56
Lady Juliana (ship), 10
Lakeman, Agnes, 3
Lambing Flat, 99, 100–1
land rights, 162–4
Lanney, William, 54, 59
League of Nations, 210
Leichhardt, Ludwig, 64, 65

Index

Letterman, David, 280
Lilley, Nathaniel, 12
Lilly (Aborigine), 134, 148
Link-Up, 163
Logan, Kim, 217
Logan, Patrick, 63
Lotus Flower Tower, 214–15

Mabo, Eddie, 164
Mabo judgement, 164
MacGillivray, John, 73, 78, 79, 80
Mackenzie, Roddy, 216
Majdanek concentration camp, 208
Malchov concentration camp, 195
Maloga, 157
Mangerner (Aborigine), 31, 33, 34
Mannapackername (Aborigine), 51
Mardudjara people, 154
Margaret (Marika Weinberger's friend), 193, 195, 198
Maroney, Karin, 264, 268
Maroney, Lindy, 264, 268, 271
Maroney, Michael, 264, 271, 272, 277, 278
Maroney, Norm, 264
Maroney, Pauline, 264, 267–8, 271–2, 275, 277–9, 282
Maroney, Sean, 264, 278
Maroney, Susie, 264–84
  begins swimming, 264–5
  wins Long Beach marathon, 265
  swims around Manhattan Island, 265–6
  swims English Channel, 266–71, 270
  swims from Cuba to US, 272–80, 278
  swims from Jamaica to Cuba, 281
  swims from Mexico to Cuba, 281
  suffers breakdown, 282–3
  receives honours, 283
  works for charities, 283
  Olympic ambassador, 263, 283–4
Martin, James, 4, 12, 19, 25, 26, 28
Martin, Marizles see Wirth, Mary Elizabeth Victoria
Martin, Polly, 140
Mary-Anne (Aborigine), 54
Matilda (Aborigine), 48, 49–50
Mauthausen concentration camp, 204
McKay, Alexander, 39
Meeks, Ouika, 118
Melrose, Constable, 134
Mengele, Josef, 181–2, 209
Mew, Sergeant, 77
Miles, Cathy, 240, 241
Miles, Katy, 240
Miles, Ron, 241, 244, 258
Miles, Samantha, 240, 241–62, 256
  education, 241–2, 259
  diagnosed with leukaemia, 243–4
  undergoes chemotherapy, 245–7, 251–5
  has lung haemorrhage, 247–9
  loses hair, 249, 255
  cancer goes into remission, 250
  kept in isolation, 250
  suffers pleurisy, 251
  has bone-marrow transplant, 253–6
  takes year off, 257
  writes book, 257, 259
  develops anorexia, 258–9
  becomes an editor, 259
  aftermath of illness, 260–1
Mimi-Ali (Aborigine), 133, 134, 135
Moore, David, 80
Moore River Native Settlement, 132–3, 136–41, 138, 159
Moorina, 32
Morton, William, 12, 13, 16, 19, 24

Mossad, 209
Mount Arapiles, 216
Mount Elbrus, 224
Mount Everest, 216–17, 222, 225–6, 229–37
Mount Kilimanjaro, 222
Mount Kosciuszko, 224
Mount Lhotse, 234
Mount McKinley, 221–2
Mount Shivling, 218
Mount Vinson, 227–9
Muir, Brigitte, 212–39
  caving experiences, 212–13
  early mountaineering experiences, 213–16
  expedition to India, 216
  marriage to Jon Muir, 216–17, 223
  trip to Gangotri, 218–19
  expedition to Gasherbrum Two, 219–21
  climbs Mount McKinley, 221–2
  climbs Mount Kilimanjaro, 222
  climbs Aconcagua, 223
  climbs Mount Elbrus, 224
  climbs Mount Kosciuszko, 224
  climbs Shisapangma, 211, 227
  climbs Mount Vinson, 227–9
  climbs Mount Everest, 225–6, 229–38, 237
  writes book, 238
Muir, Jon, 216–18, 222–3, 225–6, 229–30, 233
Munich Agreement, 203
Muralag, 68, 69–70, 81
Musgrave, Rebecca, 104
Musgrave, Sarah White, 82, 83–107, 105
  early life at Burrangong, 85–94
  endures drought and flood, 94–7
  marries Denis Regan, 97
  gives birth to two daughters, 98
  visits mother in Victoria, 98–9
  becomes a widow, 102
  meets bushrangers, 103–4
  marries Thomas Musgrave, 104
  moves to Sydney, 104–5
  death, 105
  family history, 106–7
Musgrave, Thomas, 104
Musgrave, Wallace, 104

Nazis, 203–4
Nellie (Aborigine), 133, 134
Nepean, Evan, 21
Neville, AO, 149
New South Wales Marine Corps, 11
Newgate Prison, 20
Nichols, Ross, 227
Norfolk Island, 10
Norgay, Tenzing, 218
Nottle, Craig, 217
Nuenonne people, 31, 33
Nuremberg War Tribunal, 209

O'Donohoe, Lowitja, 161
Olga (aunt of Marika Weinberger), 167, 178, 180, 182, 183, 187
O'Meally, John (bushranger), 103
Oyster Cove, 51–4, 52

Pagerly (Aborigine), 33, 34, 36, 39, 40, 43, 45
Palm Island, 159
Pandora (ship), 18
Paraweena (Aborigine), 32–3
Peaqui (Aborigine), 69, 81
Pennemukeer people, 40
Perkins, Charles, 160–1
Pevay (Aborigine), 41, 44, 48, 49–50
Phillip, Arthur, 5, 6–7, 8, 25

Index

The Pilbara, 153–5, 161
Piraprez, Camille, 214, *215*
Point Macleay, 157
Port Essington, 64
Pottle, Frederick, 26
Powlett, Commandant, 49
Prague, 195–6
Prince of Wales Island, 68, 69–70, 81

rabbit-proof fence, Western Australia, 130–1, 142
Rattlesnake (ship), *61*, 72–4, 78, 79, 80
Ravensbrück concentration camp, 193–5, 204
Rawson, Geoffrey, 26
Rawson, Lieutenant, 49
Regan, Denis, 95–6, 97, 98–9, 102
Regan, Denis James, 102
Regan, Eliza, 98, 102
Regan, George, 102
Regan, Harriet, 96
Regan, Harriet, junior, 98, 102, 104
Regan, John, 95–6, 97
Regan, William, 96
Regan, William, junior, 95–6, 97, 98, 102
Reich, Zoli, *173*
Rembang (ship), 18
Renford, Des, 267
Resolution (ship), 56
Riga, 186
Riggs, Constable, 133
Ringling Brothers Circus, 117, 125–6
Ringling, John, 117, 118–19, 123, 125
Robert (brother of Truganini), 32
Roberts, James, 101
Robertson, Jane, 95

Robinson, Charles, 36
Robinson, George Augustus, 31, 33–48, 50, 53, 58
Rogers, Will, 117
Royal Commission into Aboriginal Deaths in Custody, 163
Russia, in World War II, 204, 205, 208

Sachenhausen concentration camp, 204
Saunders, John, 200
Schreiber, Baptista, 124
Scotchie (bushranger), 86–7
Scott (seaman), 77
sealers, 41, 57
Second Fleet, 10–11
selectors, 101–2
Shisapangma, 227
Sibi (Aborigine), 75
Silver Queen (horse), 115–16
Simms, John, 12, 19, 24
Simpson, John William, 79
Singleton, George, 106
Sirius (ship), 10
Slovakia, 167–8
Smit, Detmer, 12, 13
Spence, Charlotte, 5, 12, 13, 16, 18–19, 19, 24
Spence, Mr (convict), 5
squatters, 101–2
St Leon, Phil, 117, 125, 127
Stanley, Owen, 73, 80–1
stolen generation, 132, 156–65
Stutthof concentration camp, 190–1
Suke (Aborigine), 58
Supply (ship), 10, 11
Sweetman, Al, 221–2

Tarerenorerer (Aborigine), 40
Tasman, Abel Jantzen, 56

Taylor, Frederick, 101, 102
Taylor-Smith, Shelley, 265
Tench, Watkin, 25
Thompson, Barbara Crawford, 62–81
　early life, 62
　moves to Moreton Bay, 62–4
　shipwrecked, 65–7
　lives with Torres Strait Islanders, 69–75
　rescued by crew of English ship, 76–9
Thompson, Stacey, 263
Thompson, William, 62, 64–5, 65
Timmy, Robert (Aborigine), 48, 49–50
Timor, 16
Tomagugu (Aborigine), 68, 72, 74, 76, 77, 78
Torres Strait Islanders, 15, 65–72, 74–8, 81, 163, 164
transportation, 3–7
Truganini, 30, 31–60
　life before white settlement, 31–2
　disruption of family, 32–3
　taken to Hobart, 34
　marriages, 35, 51, 54
　with Robinson on Friendly Mission, 35–45
　taken to Flinders Island, 45–6, 51
　in Victoria, 46–9
　tried in Melbourne, 50
　taken to Oyster Cove, 51, 53–4
　moves into Dandridge household, 54–5
　death, 55
　fight over remains of, 59–60
Turner, Darren, 265

Ungvar Hebrew Gymnasium, 171–2
Urdzanna (Aborigine), 70, 72, 74

Vilna Ghetto, Poland, 206

Waaksamheyd (ship), 11–12
Walyer (Aborigine), 40, 41
Warangesda, 157
Warsaw Ghetto, Poland, 206
Waterworth, Eliza, 85
Wave Hill (station), 162
Weinberger, Alex, 198–9, 200, 201
Weinberger, Catherine, 200
Weinberger, George, 200
Weinberger, Harry, 199
Weinberger, Manci, 199
Weinberger, Marika Cierer, 166, 167–202, 173
　life before the war, 167–8, 168
　high-school years, 169–70, 171
　forcibly moved to ghetto, 175–7
　on train to Auschwitz, 177–80
　at Auschwitz, 179–86
　avoids selection by Mengele, 182
　at Kaiserwald, 186–9
　at Stutthof, 190–1
　at Glöwen, 191–3
　at Ravensbrück, 193–5
　at Malchov, 195
　liberated by Russians, 196
　returns to Slovakia, 197–8
　marries, 198
　moves to Paris, 199
　migrates to Australia, 199–200, 201
Weinberger, Yvonne, 200, 202
White, Charles, 106
White, Eliza, 85, 86, 88–90, 92, 95, 97–8
White, Frank, 116, 119, 125, 126, 127
White, George, 88
White, James, 83–9, 91–4, 98–9, 101, 104, 106, 107
White, Janetta, 101

Index

White, John, 85, 88, 106–7
White, Joseph, 106
White, Sarah, 89
White, Thomas, 89, 99, 104, 106
Whitton, Thomas, 86–7
Willabi (Aborigine), 132, 142
Willocks, Don, 147–8
Wilson, Sir Ronald, 164
Wiradjuri people, 84
Wirth, George, 116–17
Wirth, Mary Elizabeth Victoria, 111, 114, 117–19, 121, 123, 125, 127
Wirth, May Zinga, 109–28
  early life, *108*, 109–10
  joins Wirth family, 110–12
  joins Wirth's Circus, 113–14
  debut as contortionist, 114
  learns trick riding, 114–16, *120*
  leaves for America, 117
  auditions for Ringling Brothers, 118–19
  performs at Madison Square Gardens, 120–1
  tours America, 121
  suffers serious falls, 122–3
  tours Britain and France, 124
  returns to Australia, 124–5
  tours with Ringling Brothers, 125–6
  retires, 126
  death, 127
  stamp commemoration, *127*, 128
Wirth, Philip, 114
Wirth, Stella, 112–13, 117, 126, 127
Wirth's Circus, 112, 120, 124, 125–7
Wonder Zoo, 124
Woorraddy (Aborigine), 33, 34–5, 36, 39, 41, 44, 51
Wybalenna, 45–6, 51

Young, 83, 101, 105

Susan Geason was born in Tasmania and grew up in Queensland. She has a BA in History and Politics from the University of Queensland, and an MA in Political Philosophy from the University of Toronto. She has worked as a Cabinet Adviser in the NSW Premier's Department and as Literary Editor of the *Sun-Herald*, and now writes for a living. She has just started a PhD in Creative Writing at the University of Queensland.

Her five novels and a collection of short stories have been published in Australia, France and Germany, and she has had short stories published in Australia, Europe and North America. Her previous non-fiction books include *Regarding Jane Eyre* and *Great Australian Girls*.

Susan Geason lives in Sydney. You can contact her at susan@susangeason.com and visit her website at www.susangeason.com